IT'S A MATTER OF THE
Heart

REV. DR. MARILYN MCCLAIN

www.TrueVinePublishing.org

It's A Matter of the Heart
Rev. Dr. Marilyn McClain

Published by True Vine Publishing Co.
810 Dominican Dr.
Nashville, TN. 37228
www.TrueVinePublishing.org

ISBN: 978-1-962783-90-3 Paperback
ISBN: 978-1-962783-02-6 eBook

DEDICATIONS

This book is dedicated to the men and women who suffer from long term effects of childhood or domestic abuse, neglect and maltreatment, who desire to break free from those affects which has caused an unhealthy state of your physical, mental, emotional, and spiritual well-being.

For all who read this book, may the words written open up the prison doors that have kept you in chains and bring healing for your body, soul and spirit."

I also make this dedication of devotion to God the Father and our Savior and Lord, Jesus Christ by the power of the Holy Spirit who set me on this path for His glory to the blessing of others.

FOREWORD

Having taught for many years, I've witnessed students come and go through my classroom. I have them for what feels like fleeting moments, and then they're off to engage in various ministries. If I've done my job well, I've shaped their understanding and kindled a desire in their hearts to seek and live out the truth of the Kingdom of God. Some students, however, possess such a hunger for knowledge that their presence in the classroom yields twofold benefits. They learn, and for the teacher, they become a cherished reward for teaching. These students swiftly become close to the heart of a professor, and their impact is equally enduring. Marilyn McClain is one such student for me.

Marilyn entered my classroom as a stranger. I knew nothing of her story or struggles; however, it didn't take long to discern something special in Marilyn's approach. Her work consistently demonstrated that finding the correct answer wasn't sufficient. Contemplation was always present, and it was evident that she wasn't merely grasping the material, but rather, she was applying and adapting as she learned. I can think of no greater satisfaction for a teacher than to witness their efforts transform the life of a student.

Marilyn's work in this book is a reflection of what I have described. You will find a tenacious and caring soul that is constantly seeking and finding truth. Her approach is simple yet profound and full of practical applications that can lead her readers to find and walk in truth and freedom. No life or struggle is a waste in the hands of a redeeming God. Marilyn's struggle was real and heart-wrenching, but through the pages of this book, she offers a way to the freedom her own self-work has brought. If you struggle or know someone who does, this book offers the hope of God's redeeming power. I am grateful to have been a small part of Marilyn's journey as one of her professors, but equally grateful for the blessing of knowing her as a cherished student.

-Dr. Steve Baggett, Emmanuel Bible College

PREFACE

I am writing this book from the depths of my heart, inspired by God's urging. As a woman who has endured childhood trauma, maltreatment, and spousal abuse from my ex-husbands, I feel compelled to convey two important messages. First, you are not alone, and it's perfectly alright to be transparent, even if it leaves you feeling vulnerable at times. Second, through the boundless grace of God, you can lead an abundant life, regardless of the enduring effects that trauma may have on your emotional, mental, and spiritual well-being. Third, as He did with me, God can employ writing or journaling as a part of your healing journey. Lastly, it's crucial for you to recognize and embrace the immeasurable value and worth you hold in the heart of your Creator, Almighty God.

Some who have faced Childhood Trauma Experiences (CTEs) or endured abuse from an intimate partner, in one form or another, refer to themselves as survivors, typically implying that they did not succumb to death. However, many of them still grapple with the enduring effects in their daily lives, often without even realizing it. But for me, I made a conscious choice not just to survive, but to break free from the shackles of those effects. This book is not about exposing others or shedding light on their experiences. Instead, it's about allowing God to reveal myself to me, for my own betterment. Blessed be His Holy Name!

So, I am elated to share with you that by the grace and power of my Creator God, I have chosen to thrive, not merely survive. This is my prayer for everyone who reads my book—that you open your heart to let the power of God permeate your being, to the extent that you, too, begin to thrive, and in turn, help others you may encounter to do the same. Know this: Our God loves you more than you can fathom!

In this book, I will attempt to bring a profound sensitivity to a diverse subject and inspire a desire within you to go deeper within yourself to find absolution regarding your life's purpose and the circumstance of living with the long-term effects of childhood trauma or domestic violence. Everything we encounter in life impacts who we are, our psychosocial health, our interpersonal skills, our personality, and our relation to and relationship with God. Understanding these elements is essential to our very core and how we identify within them is fundamental to our very existence.

This book includes an investigative study of the long -term effects of abuse, neglect, and maltreatment on the victim which is carried into adulthood and impacts every relationship. The cause may be the result of mistreatment or abuse in childhood, domestic violence by a partner, or some other direct or indirect traumatic event. Research was done to identify the prevalence of childhood trauma and domestic violence and how it impacts every area of the human makeup—physical, mental, emotional, and spiritual well-being over time.

As I embark on this journey of writing this book, God makes it very clear to me that all the years of journaling, writing down dreams, visions, and actual occurrences was and still is medicine for my soul's aches and pains. Even as I am writing this book, I find memories of childhood and domestic violence experiences creeping into this process, as if to say, "You thought you forgot about it, laid it to rest, and were healed, didn't you?" But I can now recognize these influencing thoughts as being the enemy's work, so, "no I have never forgotten it, but by the grace of God and the Person and Work of Jesus Christ, I am no longer a victim, but a healed and a thriving survivor." So regardless of the level or degree of trauma inflicted on the innocent, the vulnerable, and the unsuspecting, it will leave lasting effects on every aspect of your being.

I certainly recognize that life has to happen with so-called normal realities. But in a broken, and twisted world, people who are self-indulgent, lovers of themselves, accountable to no one, and take pleasure in their lustful desires, believe it's their god-given right to do so. Those who choose to inflict pain and suffering upon others, usually have a sick sort of internal logic which they believe gives them the right to do so. Unfortunately, they believe it to be reasonable and justifiable because their god is—self. As a result, there are some who become perpetrators who prey on the weak, the innocent, and the vulnerable. This infliction, however intended or unintended will have a significant impact on the lives to which it is directed.

The difference in the impact for the recipient is how we handle, process, and respond to the impact. As well as, how we allow a righteous God by His Holy Ghost power to deliver us from those effects, empowering us to take a stand in Him and flourish while being able to help others do the same. "He gives strength to the weary and increases the power of the weak."—Isaiah 40:29

It is certainly my prayer that my book will reach its intended readers and help to bring some level of comfort, peace, and ultimately wholeness healing. "Heal me, O Lord, and I will be healed; save me and I will be saved, for you are the one I praise."—Jeremiah 17:14"

ACKNOWLEDGEMENTS

I most importantly and humbly thank God our Father and the Lord Jesus Christ by the power of the Holy Spirit for the vision and power of bringing this book to fruition.

I would like to acknowledge the extraordinary support and encouragement of the Deans and Professors at the Emmanuel Theological Seminary in Nashville, TN. Most importantly Dr. Debbie Thomas and Dr. Mark McPherson were very instrumental in this project. They were so encouraging during the writing of the thesis for my Masters in Theology and the dissertation for both my Doctorate in Ministry and Ph.D.

I knew God had me on this path, but I felt so stressed and inadequate doing something I knew very little about, that I wanted to quit and do it later. They always gave me words of wisdom that inspired me to press forward. Little did I know that God would use those papers to bring forth this book. So I am eternally grateful to them and other professors there.

Once God started me on this vision in April of 2022, through my son-in-law, I was connected with Timothy Bond, CEO of True Vine Publishing Co. It has been such a joy working with him. A very talented, and personable young man whose expertise was paramount in creating and completing this project. We started working together in June 2022 and he walked with me every step of the way through weekly reviews of the manuscript which helped me stay on target and press forward. I could not have done it without him.

Of course, my family, thank you for your encouragement, excitement, and enthusiasm when you found out I was becoming a *world-changing author.*

I thank each and every person who in one way or another gave support and encouragement for the completion of this inspired project for the glory of God. May the Almighty God bless each of you richly!

TABLE OF Contents

INTRODUCTION

The problems of this world are fundamentally spiritual. Yet, we often experience them through our physical, mental, and emotional well-being, often without recognizing their spiritual root cause. There are no laws of man that can change how people act, for laws can't alter a person's heart. Similarly, no politician can enact a bill that will stop bigotry, prejudices, or violence.

There is no love powerful enough to make people abandon selfishness and self-centeredness without the love of Christ as the driving force within. Simply receiving the blessings and promises of God is not enough to establish a true relationship with Him, for we only witness His works. Thus, we may come to rely on His works rather than seeking to understand His ways. To truly know God, one must acquaint themselves with His character, His nature, His will, and His ways. There is no spiritual life without an intimate relationship with the Heavenly Father.

Only through a heart transplant by the Master Surgeon can we find the kind of peace on earth that Jesus spoke of when He said He left it for us. This peace is a reconciliation with God, granting us access to the power of the Holy Spirit, so that people may learn to live and love in harmony with God and their fellow beings. The issue with the world lies not in what people do, but rather in who they are—their character, personality, and belief systems, all stemming from the heart.

While we are created in the image of God, the freedom to make choices is included in that image. It is a divine gift given so that we may freely choose to love God, self, and others in the divineness of that image. It is unfortunate, however, that too many people choose to go their own way, living without interest in or consideration of the God of the Holy Scriptures—the Bible. When that happens then the selfishness, self-centeredness, and self-reasoning of humanity are exposed and run rampant from generation to generation.

Therefore, we are destined to reap the consequences of the choices made out of a damaged heart condition. In this book, we will examine the effects of some of those choices and the impact it has on one's life and on the lives of others around them. I will review and discuss some of my own real-life experiences and the long-lasting effects of inflicted trauma. However, what I desire is for you to see just how awesome and powerful our God is. I pray you will experience the love, compassion, grace, and mercy of the cross of Christ, His resurrection, and ascension with the Father as you venture through this manuscript.

Can adulthood bondage be the result of abuse, neglect, and maltreatment inflicted by others at an early age? How does the effects of spousal abuse affect one's lifestyle and choices made in daily situations and circumstances? How do we break free from the enemy's stronghold? What keeps us bound in emotional, mental, and spiritual bondage day in and day out, and year after year?

There are numerous studies that show persons who experienced some form of abuse, neglect, or maltreatment, at any age, are likely to develop serious emotional and mental illnesses, such as psychoses, major depression, schizophrenia, and bipolar disorder, in their adult life. Maltreatment of children, defined as any form of physical, sexual, or emotional abuse and neglect, is a global public health and human rights issue affecting more than one in three children aged under 18.

Although the physical, psychological, and behavioral consequences of child abuse and neglect weigh heavily on the shoulders of the children who experience it, the impact of maltreatment does not end there. The outcome for each child varies widely and is affected by a combination of factors. They include the child's age and developmental status at the time the maltreatment occurred, the type, frequency, duration, and severity of the maltreatment, and the relationship between the child and the perpetrator. Additionally, children who experience maltreatment often are affected by other adverse experiences (e.g., parental substance use, domestic violence, poverty), which can make it difficult to separate the unique effects of maltreatment (Rosen, Handley, Cicchetti, & Rogosch, 2018).[11]

It is important to learn how the lasting effects of traumatic events follow us throughout adulthood and virtually into all of our relationships, even with God which is manifested in so many different ways. We must learn how to recognize and identify related signs and symptoms that could potentially have us bound in an unhealthy state of well-being without knowing it.

It is at this crossroads that the effects of traumatic events, be it the result of childhood or relational abuse, must be addressed and steps taken to help reduce the impact on the life of the individual. This opens windows for creative strategies that can minimize or even prevent those challenging negative adverse effects.

No one deserves to be victimized by any type of abuse, neglect, or maltreatment in their lifetime by another human being. However, it is a problematic reality in the past, and present and will continue in the future until God brings about His final judgment upon evil and evil-doers. God has already let us know "... that the wickedness of man was great in the earth, and that every imagination of the thoughts of his heart was only evil continually." (Genesis 6:5 NKJV) According to Romans 5:12-the fallen, corrupt, or sin nature entered the world by one man, and by that one man, who was Adam, the sin nature is inherited by all men or human beings born of the male seed.

Even though God judged the generations of Noah's time with the universal flood upon the earth, without God the human soul still has the propensity to be and do evil in God's sight. As thriving survivors, the more we know, the more we understand, and the more we are sick and tired of being sick and tired, we will finally say enough is enough. When we look from within, we will be able to discern reasons for certain behaviors, attitudes, and emotions that hinder our mental and emotional well-being in adulthood.

These effects also invade our relationships. We must be better prepared to break free and help others do the same. Jesus said, "You shall know the truth and the truth shall make you free"', (John 8:32 KJV). The purpose of this book is to take a deeper dive into the devastating effects of abuse, trauma, and maltreatment and its long-term effects and understand that we were not created or designed to be victims of any kind of bondage, emotional, mental, or spiritual. God intended for His creation to be free to "... love the Lord thy God with all thy heart, and with all thy soul, and with all thy mind, and with all thy strength: this is the first commandment." (Mark 12:30 KJV).

God desires that we love as He loves, show kindness, mercy, and forgiveness as He does, and live a life worthy of His kingdom. But there are worldly barriers or issues that drive our hearts far from God, which binds us in darkness and we must break free by any means necessary. So my prayer for everyone who reads this book is to be inspired and empowered by the Spirit of God to recognize the need and develop a desire for a change in your life. A change that will flood your soul with peace as you come to understand some of the variables that played a part in your current psychological and spiritual development.

CHAPTER ONE

WHAT'S THE PROBLEM?

"Then the Lord saw. that the wickedness of man was great in the earth, and that every intent of the thoughts of his heart was only evil continually. And the Lord was sorry that He had made man on the earth, and He was grieved in His heart." Genesis 6:5-6 (NKJV)

Conventionally, the reason for violence of any kind against another person has been understood or thought to be due to negative emotions, like fear or anger. And those emotions manifest themselves as aggressive behavior when you are angry at someone or when you fear being hurt. Aggression can also be due to taking pleasure in seeing fear in others. These behaviors can be reinforced when the aggressor needs to control others or needs to feel dominant and powerful in a relationship.

These descriptions certainly fit the definition of a "bully" which is "a blustering, browbeating person especially one who is habitually cruel, insulting, or threatening to others who are weaker, smaller, or in some way vulnerable," according to Merriam-Webster. This behavior can be addictive, where the person has a strong inclination to act out the urges over, and over and over again, trying to reach that sweet high spot. Everything has a foundation, a beginning point and this includes emotions.

The scientific and medical world has studies that indicate certain hormones called "endorphins" are released in the brain when the human body engages in certain activities. They believe that these endorphins contribute to the state of emotions during activities of euphoria, sex, stress, or pain. According to the Mental Health America National Organization:

> "Studies have also shown that people with depression have overactive endorphins. Essentially, their bodies release endorphins in response to things that would not trigger a release of endorphins in people without depression. This is further proof that the receptors aren't functioning properly."[19]

In post-traumatic stress disorder (PTSD), endorphins help to relieve or reduce stress that contributes to high levels of anxiety. Studies have shown that anxiety is more likely if you have lower overall levels of endorphins. Endorphins also aid "coping" behavior in response to a stressful experience. A lack of endorphins leads to an inability to cope, which results in anxiety and panic."[19] Once these certain diagnoses are made, there are effective treatments that can be prescribed by appropriate practitioners.

This research information certainly helps to understand how a portion of the human body's physical and psychological systems work together. However, we cannot leave out the soul or spirit of man from this equation. For holistic healing to take place, every sick component of our being must be treated. While the scientific and medical world is absolute in their respective fields, God is absolute and the expert in His. This is our focus because the primary problem truly began when the door was open for evil to enter into this world. Every area of creation became corrupt in rebellion against God. All of the created order was made perfect until this point in time. "And God saw everything that He had made, and behold, it was very good...(Genesis 1:31, KJV). Mankind is the only created being in God's own image and likeness, made to be a reflection of Himself, (see Genesis 1:26-27). This image included feelings and emotions.

When man fell, that image or representation of God in man became impaired and all of the imperfections, human will, and self-centeredness came with that tainted likeness. According to Genesis 2:17, when God told Adam and Eve of the consequences of their disobedience in advance, He gave them fair warning. But it appears that they did not grasp the full understanding that they would have a fixed moral nature like God but it would be fixed in sin rather than righteousness as God intended. As a result, man could not reproduce in God's image but in his own image and likeness which included all of those fallen imperfections, according to Genesis 5:3.

Proverbs 14:12, KJV says, "There is a way which seemeth right unto a man, but the end thereof are the

ways of death". One might think that God created mankind to be a bunch of mindless robots, just following His
commands, but that's not the case at all. Being made in
God's own image, we have the ability to be faithful to
God's expectations. He has empowered us to be just and
upright in character to live according to His standards
which would manifest in our attitude and actions. Instead, we set our own standards to live by based on our
perception of right and righteousness and then expect
God to bless it. True right and righteousness are only determined by what's morally good and acceptable in God's
eyes. God has set the standards for all relationships –
those with Him and those with others.

God desires that we live and make all our decisions
under His grace and power of righteousness rather than
live without Him making up our own standards to live by
as we move through this life. Why? Because God in all
His infinite wisdom, knew what we would do to ourselves if left to our own moral compass. He was right
because we are still dealing with those adverse effects
today.

According to the National Domestic Violence Hotline website, domestic violence (also referred to as intimate partner violence (IPV), dating abuse, or relationship
abuse) is a pattern of behaviors used by one partner to
maintain power and control over another partner in an
intimate relationship. Domestic violence doesn't dis-
criminate. People of any race, age, gender, sexuality, re-

ligion, education level, or economic status can be a victim—or a perpetrator—of domestic violence. That includes behaviors that physically harm, intimidate, manipulate, or control a partner, or otherwise force them to behave in ways they don't want to, including through physical violence, threats, emotional abuse, or financial control. Multiple types of abuse are usually present at the same time in abusive situations, and it's essential to understand how these behaviors interact so you know what to look for. When we know what these types of relationships look like and what they mean, we can take steps to get help and help others create a path to safety and healing. [2]

The Problem Defined

Let's go straight to the heart of the matter. What rages in a heart without the loving grace, mercy, and compassion of a Holy and Righteous Judge to weigh its merits and motives? What is the human heart capable of if not kept in check?

Jesus has already explained to us in Matthew 15:17-19, that it is not what we put in our bodies that defiles us, but instead, it is what comes out of our hearts. Our pride, arrogance, and self-centeredness are all results of our fallen nature. Our personality and character manifest the reality of who we are in our hearts. We can be kind as long as things are going our way. But what happens when situations make us angry, cause us pain, or do not have positive immediate outcomes?

There is a sickness of the human heart that will allow one person to abuse another simply because they choose to. When in a relationship, the partner who chooses to bring this kind of hurt, harm, and havoc upon the other will make all kinds of excuses that sound legitimate in their own heart. For them, assaulting and battering their partner is warranted. This same damaged heart condition will allow family members to choose to abuse, neglect, and mistreat their children. These young and vulnerable children who should expect love, nurturing, and protection find themselves in households full of danger, hatred, and brutality. As a result, most of them end up living a life having to deal with long-term effects and scars from all the trauma.

Traumatic Events: Defined & Prevalence

There are many age-old questions that has been asked thousands of times in every generation. Some are "What's the problem that so many marriages end in divorce?" So many family relationships are dysfunctional. There are so many situations of people who beat, abuse, and misuse other people so easily without remorse. Why is there so much hatred, prejudice, and discrimination in the world? Why is there so much evil and wickedness in the world? And if God is so good and loving, why won't He fix this messed-up world?

I could go on and on, but these are questions that perplex the rich and the poor, every culture and nation, every believer and unbeliever alike. The viewpoint of wickedness in varying cultures and societies is often determined by where they live, whether they are wealthy or poor, and even their intellectual backgrounds.

I believe it is the desire of every human being to live a healthy, happy life in a well-established, successful career with a great family in a nice neighborhood—the typical American dream, as it has been called. According to a 2017 Pew Research Center survey on the areas of life that are universally associated with higher life satisfaction: health, your partner, career, and friends represented the most important things in life, (see Table 1.)

TABLE 1

Four areas of life universally associated with higher life satisfaction

Average life satisfaction rating among those who mentioned ____ when describing what gives them meaning in life

All four	8.4 ○
Health	7.3 ○
Spouse/Partner	7.2 ○
Career	7.1 ○
Friends	7.1 ○
None of the four	6.3 ○

5	6	7	8	9	10

Note: These differences persist in a statistical model that controls for demographic factors and response length and tests the associations between mentioning one of 30 topics in an open-ended response and respondents' life satisfaction ratings on a 0-10 scale. The shaded region represents the standard error of each estimate, a measure of uncertainty.
Source: Survey conducted Sept. 14-28, 2017, among U.S. adults.

PEW RESEARCH CENTER

According to this research, it would seem that if more of the human race would learn how to better manage their health, and make good decisions when choosing a mate, a career, and friends life would be great and this world would be a better place to live. As we review and digest data collected and analyzed, we also understand that these sample studies only take the pulse of an issue, however, the results are usually a pretty good picture of the universal thought. However, as I reviewed the research, I could not help but wonder why there were no answers that included our Creator God, religion, or spirituality that rated high enough to get counted in the final results.

And yet another survey conducted by Pew Research Center in 2021 regarding the question, "Why do bad things happen?" reports that four of the top seven responses relate to either our Creator God, religion, or spirituality. The responses reflect a vast dichotomy between the issues from far ends of the spectrum yet one seems to address the other with no one taking personal accountability. See Table 2

Many Americans say terrible experiences are just an inevitable part of life

% of U.S. adults who say terrible things happen to people through no apparent fault of their own because ...

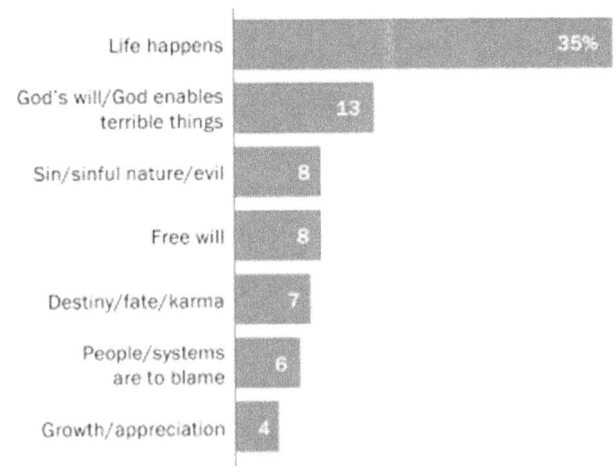

Life happens	35%
God's will/God enables terrible things	13
Sin/sinful nature/evil	8
Free will	8
Destiny/fate/karma	7
People/systems are to blame	6
Growth/appreciation	4

Note: Responses were in respondents' own words and are grouped together based on common concepts and themes. Other/unclear and DK/no response replies not shown. Results do not sum to 100% because multiple responses were permitted. Source: Survey conducted Sept. 20-26, 2021, among U.S. adults. "Few Americans Blame God or Say Faith Has Been Shaken Amid Pandemic, Other Tragedies"

PEW RESEARCH CENTER

There are numerous studies, surveys, and other data available that prove these issues of a damaged heart condition have existed for centuries, even in Biblical times, and are just as prevalent today. Unfortunately, these subject matters are extremely challenging to discuss and get out in the open because of the shame, guilt, and embarrassment it would cause them and their families. Even the church shuns these discussions or shy away from using such topics for sermons. But if those of us who have been or are affected by this revolting degradation of our whole being don't take a stand to be open and transparent how can God completely heal and mend our brokenness? Then how can we help and encourage others? How can we tell others they are not alone, that God loves them and they are important to Him? God desires that every one of us would be made whole in every area of our being because we are special. According to Psalm 139:14, God made all the delicate, inner parts of my body. He knit me together within my mother's womb. I was made wonderfully complex. God knew me as He was painstakingly designing me with much loving care.

Let us review the definitions and the prevalence of traumatic events, child abuse, and domestic violence particularly in light of co-occurrence being frequently seen in a family unit. According to www.childwelfare.gov The Federal Child Abuse Prevention and Treatment Act (CAPTA)(42 U.S.C.A. § 5106g), as amended by the CAPTA Reauthorization Act of 2010, defines child abuse and neglect as, at minimum: [4]

- Any recent act or failure to act on the part of a parent or caretaker, which results in death, serious physical or emotional harm, sexual abuse or exploitation; or

- An act or failure to act which presents an imminent risk of serious harm.

- A "child" under this definition generally means a person who is younger than age 18 or who is not an emancipated minor.

According to the World Health Organization (WHO), child abuse includes all forms of physical and/or emotional ill-treatment, sexual abuse, neglect, and negligent treatment and exploitation. In general, one distinguishes four forms of child abuse: emotional or psychological abuse, physical abuse, sexual abuse, and neglect.

The definition of domestic violence varies depending on the context in which the term is used. A clinical or behavioral definition is a pattern of assaultive and/or coercive behaviors, including physical, sexual, and psychological attacks, as well as economic coercion, that adults or adolescents use against their intimate partners.

The Office of Violence Against Women of the U.S. Department of Justice defines domestic violence as "felony or misdemeanor crimes of violence committed by a current or former spouse or intimate partner of the victim, by a person with whom the victim shares a child in common, by a who is cohabitating with or has cohabitated with the victim

as a spouse or intimate partner, by a person similarly situated to a spouse of the victim under the
domestic or family violence laws of the jurisdiction, or by any other person against an adult or
youth victim who is protected from that person's
acts under the domestic or family violence laws of
the jurisdiction."[6]

Abuse is more than bruises and broken bones. Although physical abuse and neglect leave more recogniz-
able scars, sexual, emotional, and mental abuse are just
as devastating with lasting effects. The sooner abuse is
identified, the greater the likelihood of breaking the cycle, and healing can begin in the victim's life.

Prevalence of the Problem

How much do we really know and understand about
this wickedness in our society? How can one person be
so cruel to another person? Every year, more than 3.6
million referrals are made to child protection agencies
involving more than 6.6 million children (a referral can
include multiple children). The United States has one of
the worst records among industrialized nations—losing
on average between four and seven children every day to
child abuse and neglect.

The American Society for the Positive Care of Children (American SPCC), provides the following mind-

boggling list of statistics and should move the heart of the most insensitive person:[8]

- 3.9 million child maltreatment referral reports received in 2020.
- Child abuse reports involved 7.1 million children.
- 90.6% of victims are maltreated by one or both parents.
- Only 3.1 million children received prevention & post -response services.
- Annual estimate: 1,750 children died from abuse and neglect in 2020.
- Five children die every day from child abuse.
- Sixty-eight (67.8%) percent of all child fatalities were younger than 3 years old.

The Centers for Disease Control and Prevention conducted a study on violence against children across the globe and determined that the global burden of violence against children is unknown.

"To begin to estimate the prevalence of past-year violence against children, researchers systematically reviewed data from population-based surveys and the scientific literature that included data for 96 countries on past-year prevalence of violence against children. They then used the data to develop estimates of the numbers of children in each region that had experienced violence based on data about the prevalence of violence and the size of the population of children in each region."

Key Findings were [9]

- A minimum of 50% of children in Asia, Africa, and Northern America experienced past-year violence.
- The number of 2-17-year-olds who experienced the most severe forms of violence in the past year is estimated to be at least 64% of children in Asia, 56% in Northern America, 50% in Africa, 34% in Latin America, and 12% in Europe.
- Over half of all children in the world—1 billion children ages 2-17 years-experience violence every year.

In review of this data, we can see that the seriousness of the problem is not unique to the United States.

According to statistical data from the National Coalition Against Domestic Violence for 2020:[7]

- In the United States, more than 10 million adults experience domestic violence annually.
- If each of these adults experienced only one incidence of violence, an adult in the US would experience violence every three seconds. However, because domestic violence is a pattern, many experience repeated acts of abuse annually, so an incident of abuse

happens far more frequently than every three seconds.

- 1 in 4 women and 1 in 10 men experience sexual violence, physical violence and/or stalking by an intimate partner during their lifetime with 'IPV-related impact' such as being concerned for their safety, PTSD symptoms, injury, or needing victim services
- Approximately 1 in 5 female victims and 1 in 20 male victims need medical care. Female victims sustain injuries 3x more often than male victims.
- 1 in 5 female victims and 1 in 9 male victims need legal services.
- 23.2% of women and 13.9% of men have experienced severe physical violence by an intimate partner during their lifetime.
- From 2016 through 2018 the number of intimate partner violence victimizations in the United States increased 42%.
- On a typical day, domestic violence hotlines nationwide receive over 19,000 calls. An abuser's access to a firearm increases the risk of intimate partner femicide by 400%.
- In 2018, partner violence accounted for 20% of all violent crime. Intimate partner violence is most common against women between the ages of 18-24.
- 19% of intimate partner violence involves a weapon.

Domestic violence is prevalent in every community and affects all people regardless of age, socioeconomic status, sexual orientation, gender, race, religion, or nationality. Physical violence is often accompanied by emotionally abusive and controlling behavior as part of a much larger, systematic pattern of dominance and control. Domestic violence can result in physical injury, psychological trauma, and even death. The devastating consequences of domestic violence can cross generations and last a lifetime.[7]

Prevalence of the Problem in the church

The Commission was established in 2018 after the French catholic church faced growing criticism for its handling of sexual abuse scandals. The establishment of the commission came at a time when public confidence in the church was at an all-time low and it faced dwindling congregations. The French report follows similar disclosures of sexual abuse allegations against Roman Catholic clergy members in the United States, Germany, Australia, Ireland, Poland and several others. As a result of this investigation an article in the online www.Forbes.com reports that there are around 330,000 children have been sexually abused by members of the French Catholic church since 1950, including 216,000 by priests and clergy, the independent commission said Tuesday in a report that demonstrates that sexual exploitation of minors in the church was far more severe than previously known.[10]

According to the Washington Post,

"more than 300 Catholic priests across Pennsylvania sexually abused children over seven decades, protected by a hierarchy of church leaders who covered it up, according to a sweeping grand jury report released Tuesday. The investigation, one of the broadest inquiries into church sex abuse in U.S. history, identified 1,000 children who were victims, but reported that there probably are thousands more. "Priests were raping little boys and girls, and the men of God who were responsible for them not only did nothing; they hid it all. For decades," the grand jury wrote in its report. The 18-month investigation covered six of the state's dioceses Allentown, Erie, Greensburg, Harrisburg, Pittsburgh and Scranton-and follows other state grand jury reports that revealed abuse and cover-ups in two other dioceses. The grand jury reviewed more than 2 million documents, including from the "secret archives"— what church leaders referred to the reports of abuse they hid from the public for decades, state Attorney General Josh Shapiro said at a news conference Tuesday." [11]

The Southern Baptist Convention, America's largest Protestant denomination, confronted its own sex-abuse crisis three weeks ago in the form of an investigation by the Houston Chronicle and San Antonio Express-News. The newspapers reported that hundreds of Southern Baptist clergy and staff had been accused of sexual misconduct over the past 20 years, including dozens who returned to church duties, while leaving more than 700 victims with little in the way of justice or apologies. For both denominations, allegations of cover-ups and insufficient sympathy for victims have been as damaging in the public eye as the abuse itself, [12]

It has been a wrenching season for three of America's largest religious denominations, as sex-abuse scandals and a schism over LGBT inclusion fuel anguish and anger within the Roman Catholic, Southern Baptist, and United Methodist churches. There's rising concern that the crises will boost the ranks of young people disillusioned by organized religion.

"Every denomination is tremendously worried about retaining or attracting young people," said Stephen Schneck, a political science professor at Catholic University. "The sex-abuse scandals will have a spillover effect on attitudes toward religion in general."[7]

"This article explores the effects of child sexual abuse by priests and other perpetrators on victims' trust in the Catholic Church, priesthood, and in their relationship to God. Adult Catholics (1,810) in the United States and Canada were separated into three groups: those who reported no childhood sexual abuse (N = 1,376), those who had been sexually abused as children but not by a priest (N = 307), and those who had been sexually abused by priests (N = 40). Analyses of variances compared the level of trust in priesthood, the Church, and God of these three groups and found a significant decline from those "not abused" to those "abused by a priest." There was a slight decline in trust for those "abused but not by a priest," however, the results were statistically inconclusive. The 347 victims were then separated into two groups based upon their having received psychotherapy. The "treatment" group (N = 152) reported significantly less trust in the priesthood, Church, and in their relationship to God than the "no treatment" group (N = 194). This study highlighted the possible spiritual damage caused by child sexual abuse, particularly if the perpetrator was a religious leader, and supported the need to assess the religious impact of the victim's abuse and to include a process of spiritual healing.[17]

With so much data regarding this terrible issue of violence, abuse, and maltreatment, it would seem that more Christian churches, ministries, and organizations would be more vocal, and more involved in addressing these issues.

Prevalence of the Problem in Ancient Times

The Massacre of the Innocents is the incident in the nativity narrative of the Gospel of Matthew 2:16-18 in which Herod the Great, king of Judea, orders the execution of all male children two years old and under in the vicinity of Bethlehem. The king committed several atrocities against others including his own sons and wives. Herod gave this order to capture and kill the would-be King of the Jews who might usurp his throne and power. He was hoping to get the baby that had been born in a manger as the prophecies told. Scripture does not give us a specific number of the children killed because of Herod's order but the Greek liturgy asserts that there were more than 14,000 male children found under the age of two. [12]

After the much kinder Pharaoh of Joseph's time died, a new king came to power in Egypt at the beginning of the Book of Exodus. The new Pharaoh of Exodus did not know about Joseph or his good deeds, nor did he care. Instead, he began to treat the Israelites who were Joseph's people like slaves. As the Hebrew population grew, they became a great military threat to Pharaoh.

Pharaoh developed a plan to help monitor and control the Hebrew population. He ordered the Hebrew midwives to throw all newborn Jewish males into the Nile River. Of course, they couldn't outright refuse the king. But they were God-fearing women. So they told him that the Hebrew women were so lively in childbirth that the babies were being born before they could get to them, (see Exodus 1:1-22).

Domestic violence and murder took place in the house of the father and mother of humanity. Cain killed his brother Abel out of jealousy, and envy and had no respect for God, (see Genesis 4;1 John 3:12). It's clear both brothers brought their sacrifice to God out of the condition of their hearts. Abel's sacrifice was given in sincere respect, reverence, and worship of the Lord. But Cain's sacrifice was not accepted because the motive of his heart was not right. And yet, a gracious God gave Cain an opportunity to think about his action, repent, and maybe try again in Genesis 4:6-7. Instead, the wickedness of Cain's heart caused him to respond in arrogance and hatefulness in verse 9 where Cain asks, "Am I my brother's keeper?"

The story of Joseph is another example of domestic violence of the older preying on the younger as their wicked hearts are revealed. Joseph was the beloved son of Jacob. His older brothers were so jealous of his relationship with their father that they plotted to kill Joseph, but instead, they sold him into slavery, (see Genesis 37).

They lied to their father and told him they found Joseph's coat covered with much blood but they didn't find the boy anywhere. So Jacob presumed Joseph dead and mourned him for a long time.

Finally, another heinous act against infants recorded in ancient times is child sacrifice, According to ancient history, the non-Jewish people "...built the high places of Baal, which are in the valley of the son of Hinnom, to cause their sons and their daughters to pass through the fire unto Molech; which I commanded them not, neither came it into my mind, that they should do this abomination, to cause Judah to sin," (Jeremiah 32:35 KJV).

The pagan god, Molech is usually depicted as a bull-headed statue with arms stretched out and a huge opening in its belly where they lit a raging fire which was heated until the flames were glowing. Then, as the pinnacle of pagan worship, an infant would be placed in his hands while the people, including parents, listened to the infant cry as it burned to death before their eyes. God certainly hated this as He forbade Israel to participate in this kind of worship. He tells them this is an abomination to Him and it would not even enter into His mind to request such a thing.

Time and time again, we see the depravity of the human heart and what it is capable of when left unchecked. Man will choose to do anything he deems right in his own eyes, regardless of who it hurts as long as it is self-serving and self-satisfying. There is only one way of absolution to keep your spiritual heart healthy and that is by the truths and power of God's word. Strategic applications will be discussed in later chapters of the book. When the heart is right with God and we walk in fellowship with Him, the motive that drives our thoughts and actions will be one of love, kindness, and gentleness, which is the will of God.

As you come to the end of this first chapter, I hope you are beginning to view life's issues differently as it relates to the human heart and that there is a true underlying problem that must be addressed. To have a deeper view certainly helps those of us who have been victimized to stand stronger in our walk knowing that it was never God's intention that man should be evil-doers against one another.

Father in heaven, I pray that your Holy Spirit will transform our hearts and minds by renewing us in the power of Your word. Help us to understand how to think and walk from Your perspective and not our own. Teach us how to move and have our being in Your word by Your grace as we seek healing and spiritual growth, in the mighty name of Your Son, Jesus the Christ. Amen.

CHAPTER TWO

THE PSYCHOLOGICAL EFFECTS OF TRAUMATIC EVENTS

The immediate effects of abuse, neglect or relational violence may be seen as isolation, fear, or an inability to trust others. This unhealthy emotional state can result in a lifetime of consequences such as low self-esteem, depression, and relationship difficulties, just to name a few.

According to the Office of Disease Prevention and Health Promotion organization:

"Mental disorders are among the most common causes of disability. The resulting disease burden of mental illness is among the highest of all diseases. In any given year, an estimated 18.1% (43.6 million) of U.S. adults ages 18 years or older suffered from any mental illness and 4.2% (9.8 million) suffered from a seriously debilitating mental illness. Neuropsychiatric disorders are the leading cause of disability in the United States, accounting for 18.7% of all years of life lost to 1 ten disability and premature mortality. Moreover, suicide is the 10th leading cause of death in the

United States, accounting for the deaths of approximately 43,000 Americans in 2014. [18]

Mental and emotional health problems are usually the result of a combination of many factors including unhealthy family dynamics and the impact of traumatic events such as childhood abuse or interpersonal violence. The United States Department of Health and Human Services indicates that of the 30 to 60 percent of families where spousal abuse takes place, children who witness this violence often become victims of physical abuse or neglect. Abused parents tend to be unresponsive to their children due to their own fears. Even if children are not mistreated, they experience harmful emotional disorders from the violence they witness.

Psychological effect is something that affects or arises in the mind which relates to the mental and the emotional state of a person. The effects of traumatic events on the mind are devastating to a person's well-being. This is especially true for children who are severely mistreated in any way and have not yet developed effective coping skills. While emotional health involves managing our emotions and feelings, mental health is our ability to manage our thoughts, stress, and our ability to process and understand information from life's experiences.

They are closely related, yet very different. You can have periods of anxiousness without being diagnosed with an anxiety disorder. There will be situations you encounter that may cause you grief or expressions of depression, but you may not be diagnosed with Depressive Disorder. Both disorders are mental health diagnoses usually requiring some form of treatment. But when you experience symptoms that subside once the situation has been resolved then it is more related to emotional health and usually requires no treatment. This makes it helpful to understand how significant the mental and emotional state of health can be impacted by any type of abusive trauma in our lives.

Families or individuals who have experienced domestic violence will go through a process of healing, the difference is the quality of that process. Since the trauma can have various effects on the mind, body, and spirit, the challenge in healing is its effectiveness and appropriateness. It is natural to experience the challenges of healing, and acknowledging the effects can be an important first step toward restoration. Even though survivors may experience similar types of abuse, the response to trauma will vary from person to person.

Many factors influence how a person responds to abuse, such as the frequency of occurrences, degree of severity, and the effects on physical health. The overall impact of domestic violence or childhood trauma also depends on the person's natural reactions to stress and how they cope with stressful situations. Other factors can include the age at which the trauma occurred and previous exposure to other unrelated traumatic incidents. People who are victimized by others will often experience mental, emotional, and spiritual shifts that will persist and even get worse if not identified and properly addressed. It is not uncommon for them to even have lapses of memory where they cannot recall some life experiences prior to the abuse.

These lapses can actually be periods of time where one may not remember details of certain events, whether negative or positive. One may not be able to recall things they liked to do or friends they may have had in their pre-traumatic event life. I have prayed so many times asking God to let me remember some of my childhood or teenage years, and experiences, but He hasn't done it yet. So I'm trusting His decision and timing because God knows best. Since He knows best, just maybe it's best not to remember, especially not knowing what those memories may hold.

Even though the federal government and every state has a great deal of oversight and assistance to combat child trauma and domestic violence, the percentage of incidents remains staggering. Research asserts that there are still a number of cases that go unreported or uninvestigated every year. The majority of research institutes around the world agree that the effects of abuse, neglect, and domestic violence are extremely diverse in every area of life as indicated by the following non-exhaustive list:

- Intergenerational transmission
- Re-victimization
- Physical health problems—diabetes, GI disorders, migraine headaches, gynecological issues, high blood pressure
- Mental and emotional health problems—personality disorders, PTSD, dissociative disorders, depression (most common), anxiety disorder and Bi-polar and other psychosis
- Suicidal tendencies and behavior
- Eating disorders, obesity
- Alcohol and substance abuse
- Aggression, violence, and criminal behavior
- High-risk sexual behavior, and
- Homelessness

These effects of child abuse and neglect can lead to a wide range of adverse outcomes in adulthood and are often interrelated. Experiencing chronic and multiple forms of maltreatment or victimization can increase the risk of more severe and damaging adverse repercussions in adulthood. However, the effects of violence in an adult partner relationship can be just as devastating. Most victimized adults may have developed coping skills to mask and suppress the mental and emotional impact. This type of coping can often make the healing process that much more difficult but not impossible.

Psychological Consequences: Child abuse and neglect can cause a variety of psychological problems. Maltreatment can cause victims to feel isolation, fear, and distrust, which can translate into lifelong psychological consequences that can manifest as educational difficulties, low self-esteem, depression, and trouble forming and maintaining relationships. Researchers have identified links between child abuse and neglect and the following psychological outcomes.[1]

1. **Diminished executive functioning and cognitive skills:** Disrupted brain development as a result of maltreatment can cause impairments to the brain's executive functions: working memory, self-control, and cognitive flexibility.

2. **Poor mental and emotional health**: Experiencing childhood maltreatment is a risk factor for depression, anxiety, and other psychiatric disorders throughout adulthood. Studies have found that adults with a history of ACEs had a higher prevalence of suicide attempts then those who did not.

3. **Attachment and social difficulties**: Infants in foster care who have experienced maltreatment followed by disruptions in early care-giving can develop attach-

ment disorders. Attachment disorders can negatively affect a child's ability to form positive peer, social, and romantic relationships later in life.

4. **Post Traumatic stress**: Children who experienced abuse or neglect can develop posttraumatic stress disorder (PTSD), which is characterized by symptoms such as persistent re-experiencing of the traumatic events related to the abuse; avoiding people, places, and events that are associated with their maltreatment; feeling fear, horror, anger, guilt, or shame; startling easily; and exhibiting hyper vigilance, irritability, or other changes in mood.

Mental health and illnesses can also be seen in ancient times as those recorded in the Bible. Elijah certainly experienced some fears, anxieties, and maybe some symptoms of depression as well. Those symptoms in today's language are considered effects of post-traumatic stress. A contest of the gods on Mount Carmel is recorded in 1 King 18 in which Elijah, the prophet of God and the opposing priest of Baal would prove which god was alive and most powerful. Which god would rain down fire from heaven and consume the sacrifice to prove who was superior?

Elijah challenged 450 prophets of Baal so the people could see that the God of Israel was the only Living and True God. This would convince the people to trust God

Rev. Dr. Marilyn McClain

and turn their hearts back to Him. The prophets of Baal did all they could: dancing, praying, and self-mutilating all day to get Baal to respond, to no avail. Elijah readjusted the altar stones, added a lot of water to the altar and then he prayed according to 1 Kings 18:30-39. Then the fire of the Lord rained down from heaven. It consumed the sacrifice, burnt up the wood, the stones, and the dust, and licked up every drop of water. The Living God will always prove who He is for us to trust and have faith in Him.

After the contest was done, God told Elijah to kill all 450 prophets of Baal, not even one should escape. At that time in the pagan world, Baal was perceived to be supreme and the most powerful of all the gods. Elijah followed God's instructions. At a time when Elijah should have been excited about God's victory and should have drawn strength from it, it appears Elijah begins to think more about what Jezebel was going to do when she finds out what happened.

In 1 Kings 19 when Jezebel heard of the slaughter of Baal's 450 prophets, she angrily swore to have Elijah killed within the next 24 hours. Even though God proved He was the only True and Living God for Elijah, and allowed him to kill all the prophets of Baal without being harmed, Jezebel was still a very dangerous threat. Verse three tells us that Elijah was so terrified, that he ran hard and long toward Beer-Sheba in Judah. He had his servants with him, they all were running. This was not an

51

overnight run. The approximate distance from Jezreel to Beer-Sheba is about one hundred miles.

Can you imagine running in fear for your life, knowing that if you stop to eat, drink, or sleep, the enemy may pounce on you and probably all those with you? Even though Elijah was fit enough to run almost twenty miles in the rain, ahead of King Ahab's chariots in 1 Kings 18:45-46, running in fear for your life for one hundred miles or so, is something else. Scripture doesn't tell us how long it took Elijah to get to Beer-Sheba, but certainly, his physical condition reflected the drive.

It's almost certain he was emaciated, with signs of dehydration and malnutrition; his skin dry and sagging, his lips pale, dry and cracked. He had to be dirty with foul odors. What a mess he must have been. After arriving at Beer-Sheba, he left his servants there and went farther into the desert alone, no doubt to die as we see in verse four. However, God shows up for Elijah proving that even though we will endure agony, pain, and suffering in this life at the hands of others or because of our own choices, He does promise to help us through it.

Perhaps Elijah had come to expect the spiritual high life of supernatural events and was not ready for such a scary dimension of service to God. But it seems Elijah could not shake the emotional and mental stress posed by the fear of Jezebel's threat. She was a vicious and ruthless adversary, and Elijah knew it. Only a short time had passed since another prophet of God, Obadiah, had told him about the massacre of God's prophets at the hand of Jezebel during her reign of terror. Maybe Elijah even knew some of those prophets who were brutally murdered and it all came rushing back to his memory as he ran for his life. This had to add to the impact of his post-traumatic stress situation. Elijah was at his wits end with fear and anxiety.

He ran hard and fast until he was so physically and mentally exhausted, he couldn't go any further. He found himself in the desert under a juniper tree, despondent, defeated, and depressed. He prayed, asking God to take his life. Surely he would rather his loving God kill him than brutal Jezebel. He was in such bad shape mentally and emotionally, that he was praying for death to come. However, most people really don't want to die, they just want the pain to stop.

In 1 Kings 19:5 -18, we see how God steps in, sends an angel to provide for Elijah's physical, mental, and emotional needs, and assures him he is not alone. God miraculously provided bread and water for Elijah by sending an angel to give him food and drink over and over. Elijah was so out of it, that God's angel had to wake him up again and again just to get him to eat and drink. He rose up, ate the meal, and passed right back out. Symptoms of depression will cause loss of appetite, a desire to just sleep, and a lack of the will to live. But his compassionate God didn't let Elijah give up.

God protected and provided for his physical, mental, and emotional needs over the next forty days and nights while Elijah traveled to Mount Horeb, the Mountain of God. Seeing that God allowed Elijah to wander in the desert those forty days and nights, undoubtedly reminded him of Moses and the children of Israel following the exodus from Egypt. This had to give some revival to the heart and mind of Elijah remembering how God took care of the Israelites, never leaving or forsaking them. While in the cave of the mountain, God and Elijah had a conversation.

Elijah is complaining about his devotion to God, and telling God how he is the last of the great prophets while at the same time really putting down the children of Israel. In his self-righteous spirit, he continued bragging about being the only one left to go through these hardships, but of course, God had to show him he was wrong, in the remaining verses 19 to 21 of this chapter. God responded, telling Elijah to go out of the cave and stand on the mountain, but Elijah did not go out. God proceeded to send a wind storm upon the mountain, then an earthquake and a raging fire in rapid succession, but none of those violent storms brought Elijah out of the cave.

Out of God's compassion and grace, He was trying to get Elijah to slow down, release his fears, and remember who God is and what God has already done. After Elijah's initial responses of fear, complaining, and self-righteousness, and the turbulent storms sent by God, he finally hears the small voice of God as stated in verse 13. Elijah now finds the strength and courage to reset his mental, emotional, and spiritual position as he prepares to persevere with the work of the Lord. It was God's gracious voice that caused him to get up, wrap in his mantle, and go outside the cave as God instructed.

Many times when we hear the voice of God, we don't really listen. The Hebrew word for "hear" is shema (shuh-mah'). Some form of the word hear is used more than 1300 times in the King James Bible which is an indication of its significance. The majority of the use of the word "hear", instructs the listener to give undivided attention; understand and obey; and gain or get knowledge to take action. Regardless of the situation, we cannot allow the evil actions of others to dictate the level of our trust and faith in Almighty God.

According to the APA Dictionary of Psychology, demon possession is:

"the supposed invasion of the body by an evil spirit or devil that gains control of the mind or soul, producing mental disorder, physical illness, or criminal behavior. Many forms of physical and psychological illness were formerly attributed to such possession, notably epilepsy, schizophrenia, and Tourette's disorder."[23]

Let's look at another event that is recorded in the Bible, Mark 5:1-20. The occurrence of the man under demonic possession and influence presents a great number of psychological issues. This man's whole being was being controlled by demonic forces, which made him a terror to society. We find him living in the tombs of the Gerasenes mountains on the east side of the Sea of Galilee. He's so out of his mind that he's running around naked and mutilating himself. He was a social outcast. He had absolutely no control over his psychological state during this time. Every effort to restrain him failed.

When the townspeople tried to help by binding him up with shackles and iron chains, he would overtake them and break loose. Because of his demonically inspired strength no one could subdue him. He was so messed up mentally and emotionally, he endured self-inflicted agony as he cried out all hours of the day and night. This man battled with a number of conditions such as paranoia, psychotic episodes, mental torment by the demons, self-inflicted physical injury, isolation, and fear of others. Can you imagine having absolutely no control of any area of your psyche and you know it but can't do anything about it?

Then the day came when Jesus went into the country of the Gadarenes and met the man out of the tombs. The demons caused the man to fall at Jesus' feet as they recognized His power and authority over him. In that same hour, Jesus cast out every demon that had possession over the man's body. This Jesus Christ encounter brought about a holistic healing for this man, one such that no other power could do.

The prophet Isaiah spoke about the mission of the coming Messiah in Isaiah 61:1 NKJV, "The Spirit of the Lord God is upon Me, Because the Lord has anointed Me To preach good tidings to the poor; He has sent Me to heal the brokenhearted, To proclaim liberty to the captives, And the opening of the prison to those who are bound."

A closer look reveals the work of the coming Lord who will bring joy to those who are poor in spirit, to heal the sick, and brokenhearted, to free us from the clutches of sin and demonic forces. In both events, God's prophet, Elijah and his fear of Jezebel and the demon-possessed man healed by Jesus, we find examples of the psychological effects of traumatic events and the significant impact on a person's mental, emotional and spiritual well-being. But we also see that in both cases only God could bring about complete healing. So these issues or conditions are not new. We must learn to discern the real problem and apply the real treatment solution—the Power of the Messiah, the Christ, the Anointed One.

Oh Lord, my Father in heaven, as I review this chapter of the book it is a profound section because of the content. Help us to understand what it all means and how to allow Your compassion and loving kindness to set us free from the shackles and chains that bind our body, our mind and our spirit. In Jesus name, Amen.

CHAPTER THREE
SPIRITUAL EFFECTS OF TRAUMATIC EVENTS

Traumatized survivors' identities and self-images are often marred and shattered by abuse. Their connection to themselves, others, and God becomes distorted and broken. This creates a great catechism between their pre and post-abuse ways of living and spiritual views. This maltreatment not only imposes trauma on the victims' bodies, it also negatively impacts their perspectives and relationships with God. The violation of physical, mental, and relational boundaries may immediately trigger a spiritual crisis.

What is a spiritual crisis? What does it look like? The Spiritual crisis or spiritual emergency is recognized by the American Psychiatric Association as a distinct psychological disorder that involves a person's relationship with a transcendent being or force; it might be accompanied by assumptions related to meaning or purpose in life.

"The disorder may be accompanied by any combination of the following symptoms, which include feelings of depression, despair, loneliness; loss of energy or chronic exhaustion not linked to a physical disorder; loss of control over one's personal and/or professional life; unusual sensitivity to light, sound, and other environmental factors; anger, frustration, lack of patience; loss of identity, purpose, and meaning; withdrawal from life's everyday routines; feelings of madness and insanity; a sense of abandonment by God; feelings of inadequacy; estrangement from family and friends; loss of attention span, self-confidence, and self-esteem; and frequent bouts of spontaneous crying and weeping."

For those who profess to be Christian and know God, as they recall those traumatic experiences, they may begin to question God: His power, His love, His sovereignty, and even His very existence. Additionally, during this urgent period, other questions may come up. Some of these may be "Why am I really here?"; "What is my purpose?"; and "How can I really find the answers?" When these situations happen, the mind is so confused that the person may not even be able to get their thoughts under control which can lead to a psychotic breakdown. This profound crisis in the individuals' faith and trust in God and others can be so devastating that it can lead to suicidal behavior.

For those who survive the experiences, what they believe about God may be so distorted, that it can take a lifetime for God to tear down and break through the barriers of the heart and mind. Those barriers may include hostility, hatred, bitterness toward God, and even complete alienation from God. But God is compassionate, gracious, and longsuffering, (see Exodus 34:6). God will take all the time necessary to tear down walls and break through any barriers built up because of the wicked acts inflicted by others.

Abusive trauma can lead to starvation of the spirit. It is less obvious than physical hunger because it can not be seen from the outside. It has a much slower effect, and it can be hidden away easier. It is easier to cover up guilt and shame of what's going on behind closed doors. They may stop attending Bible study, worship service, or other church activities.

When a living thing falls from what gives it life, it dies. As I watch the leaves fall from the trees in my yard, they dry up, become brittle, and blow away. There is no way to reconnect that leaf with its source of life because it was completely severed. There was another young tree whose branch was split from the trunk and when a splint was put in place to reattach it to the tree, it began to show signs of life again.

If you have never had a relationship with God through Christ Jesus, you are like the leaf that blows away in a spiritual crisis. You have lost your connection to the Source of life and strength. But those who are in Christ and Christ in them, never lose spiritual life again because you are sealed and splinted by the power of the Holy Spirit that keeps you attached. Our minds are the greatest assets we have and the Giver of that asset should be given priority when it is threatened.

Many people believe the reason for moral impurity and spiritual crisis is the attack of the enemy. Some believe that all evil is a result of demonic possession. The enemy, of course, is that old serpent in the Garden, called Satan. Yes, we do know that he is real, and he does have a level of power given to him by God. We also know that he hates God and has always desired to be greater than God. The Bible reveals the heart of Satan is like the one mentioned in Isaiah 14:12-14,

"How you are fallen from heaven, O Lucifer, son of the morning! How you are cut down to the ground, you who weakened the nations! For you have said in your heart: 'I will ascend into heaven, I will exalt my throne above the stars of God: I will also sit on the mount of the congregation On the farthest sides of the north; I will ascend above the heights of the clouds, I will be like the Most High."

Clearly, his intent and desire can be understood. The Bible teaches that the Devil is like a thief who comes to steal, kill, and destroy the relationship between God and His people, (see John 10:10). From Genesis to Revelations, he continuously attempts to ensnare God's people, enticing them to reject anything godly, especially the true word of God. Satan wants to destroy the body of Christ which is every born-again believer. As Jesus told Peter, in Luke 22:31, "Satan desires to have you that he may sift you like wheat." The Church, created by God, cannot be destroyed but its members (the believers) can be influenced and attacked which hinders its work. Jesus declares to His disciple, Peter, in Matthew 16:18 NKJV "... on this rock I will build My church and the gates of Hades shall not prevail against it". So Satan and his demons cannot win. Jesus sealed their judgment and fate at the Cross and the Resurrection. But apparently, Satan is not willing to concede defeat just yet. He wreaks havoc in the lives of God's people. Although, much of it is because we respond to his tactics and influencing strategies, often not realizing that we give him the power to do so.

Satan has various strategies that he uses and when we are faced with mental and emotional issues for whatever reason, we certainly need to be aware of them. So we dare not minimize the power and presence of demonic forces. But we should also know his limitations. Understanding those limitations puts his power in the right perspective compared to God's power. It also helps us to discern and use the proper weapon of warfare.

When we find ourselves in a spiritual crisis, we often give too much attention and credit to the enemy, when we should be focusing our energy on seeking the One who has all power in heaven and earth. We also tend to fight a spiritual battle with carnal weapons—well guess what—they don't work. Many believe that Satan or his demons are responsible for their struggle and that they can inhabit a believer's body and mind. Satan and his demons are created angelic beings whose powers are not equal to or greater than the divine attributes of God. Though demons can enter and possess an unbeliever, they can strongly influence a believer's sinful nature and desires of the flesh through our senses, and our emotional and mental capacities. He has to attack us from the outside to influence the inside, but we don't have to give in.

The Bible helps us to understand that. "...The One who is in you (the Son of God) is greater than the one (devil) who is in the world," (1 John 4:4 NIV). Believers do not live under the authority of the power of darkness, which includes the powers and influences of this world. "He has rescued us from the dominion of darkness and brought us into the kingdom of the Son, He loves, in whom we have redemption, the forgiveness of sins." (Colossians 1:13,14 NIV).

Believers should have nothing in common with the powers of darkness, spiritual wickedness in high places, or Satan and his demonic influences. I do not believe that the Holy Spirit, and a demonic spirit, can co-exist in the same person's heart and mind. "And what harmony is there between Christ and Belial? or what does a believer have in common with an unbeliever?" (2 Corinthians 6:15 NIV). Paul also illustrates this Biblical truth well in Romans 7, and he puts the blame appropriately where it belongs, the will of his sinful nature wanting to do what it wants to do and he made the choice not to yield to it.

Only the Living God is all-knowing, all-powerful, and can be everywhere all at the same time. Satan is a created spirit being, a fallen angel, and cannot be in more than one place at a time. He can not know the thoughts and intentions of the heart and mind of man, although he is cunning enough to read our words and actions, his powers are limited. He is a want-to-be god, so stop giving him so much time and attention. Time spent focused on the devil and his demons is time lost in fellowship with God.

Why do the abused stay with or return to an abusive partner? There are no absolute answers to this question because it lies within the heart of the abused and will be different for each. However, research finds that most reasons can be placed under four broad categories which are: controlling power, manipulation, love, and hope. Abusive trauma breaks down a person's confidence. It causes an overwhelming belief that you lack the ability to cope outside the relationship and it makes you feel like you are powerless to break free.

I can recall many times in my abusive marriages when I thought about running away. I tried to plan how to leave, when to leave, and where to go. I contemplated who I could tell, who could get involved, and what would happen if I did. So many questions and so few answers make you talk yourself right out of taking any action at all. Especially when your family forces you to get married at 17 because of pregnancy. During that time it was an embarrassment and brought shame to everyone.

Back in my day, a pregnant teenager couldn't even stay in public school. You either found an adult education school or you went back to finish after the baby was born. Unfortunately, this caused many young girls to just drop out. Of course, in today's society, these issues are not the same. Today, television and social media romanticize teen pregnancy. It is not depicted as shameful or an embarrassment to families. Teenage girls are allowed to remain in public schools if they choose. Having children at any young age brings about so many challenges and hardships that most teenagers do not have the skills to handle effectively. In addition, the effects of those challenges are often negative and can lead to abusive outcomes.

As I often look back, I see what I didn't know then. God had His hand on me and my situation when I didn't even know it. He made a way and found an adult education location close enough that I could walk to which enabled me to keep up my studies. Doing that allowed me to return to my public high school and graduate on time with my class. To God be the glory!

I often wish I had known Jesus as Savior and Lord during those days. Oh, I knew God the Father, but I didn't have a relationship with Him through Christ until later years. It's because of that relationship and the experience of an intimate fellowship now that I can share with others in the hope that someone will benefit and God will get the glory.

As for those of us who have been victimized by others, we must stop and take a stand for our own health and well-being. We must stop waiting for and expecting a change of heart from the abusers. While trauma may leave us feeling powerless and fearful, it is possible to break free of these situations and move forward stronger. We must seek to be empowered through a relationship with Christ to walk in freedom.

We must understand that Almighty God who loves us so much has already ensured that our health and well-being are rooted and grounded in Him—not in man. But God will never take away or infringe on our right to free will choices. It's up to us to stand boldly in Him and make the choice of removing the chains. This, of course, includes the chains of mental and emotional long-term effects well after we have achieved physical freedom.

Physical freedom is not just being removed from one location or position to another. You must seek clinical or medical help to manage those illnesses or disorders resulting from post-traumatic stress. Your clinician may be your counselor, your Pastor, your Priest, your medical doctor, or whomever you have chosen to assist you in your healing.

Mental and emotional health is defined in detail in chapter two of this book. While they are often interrelated, a difference can be discerned in various situations.

Identifying which disorder is the most prevalent in your life will help you and your clinician to determine the most effective treatment. Learn to recognize the signs of unhealthy emotional states such as uncontrollable crying without a known reason, fear of letting others get too close in a relationship, unhealthy eating disorders, or substance abuse. These could be effects of some traumatic childhood experiences.

An unhealthy mental status can be recognized by symptoms like depression, anxiety disorders, or phobias. Are you experiencing any of these signs that you have not looked into, reported to your clinician, or talked to God about? Could they be linked to some abusive situation that affected you directly or indirectly?

Signs and symptoms like these are not normal. These are indications that something is going on in your physical, psychological, or spiritual being that need attention. Pain of any kind is always a warning bell. It sounds when the alarm goes off, shouting find it and fix it. The root cause must be identified, addressed, and properly treated for holistic healing to take place.

There is no other way to accomplish holistic healing. Understanding the truth of God's word and making practical application in our daily crisis situations is our strategic weapon of warfare given by God. We must exercise every available tool and avenue God has placed at our disposal and allow Him to employ His power in the midst.

My Father in heaven, as You continue to guide me through this therapy process of writing this book, I thank You for every detail, for every thought, and for every enlightenment that brings joy, peace, and gratefulness. I pray that every reader will digest its content, allowing You to manifest Your glory in their healing, in the mighty name of Jesus, Amen.

CHAPTER FOUR

IT'S A MATTER OF THE HEART

"Keep thy heart with all diligence; for out of it are the issues of life." Proverbs 4:23 KJV

The medical field has published multiple resources that give us tips on how to keep our physical heart healthy and strong. They tell us not to smoke or use tobacco, to eat heart-healthy foods and do routine physical exercises. Other tips include managing stress, getting quality sleep, and regular checkups. Additionally, if your practitioner diagnoses a heart problem they will generally prescribe a medication regimen. If a prescription is given, would you not get it filled and take the medicine as prescribed? While following these directions will reduce the risk of having a heart attack, it does not guarantee it. But there is a way to improve the odds of not only reducing the risks of a literal heart attack but also reducing the risks of a spiritual heart attack.

We live in a culture that has taken some biblical words and used them in a way that redefines and cheapens the message because it distorts God's intended meaning. The word "heart" is used over 830 times in the King James version of the Bible. We need to break down how it's used in the Bible to get the full significance of its meaning. Let's look at some of the ways the Bible talks about this word.

The Biblical view of the heart is as the control center of your personality; your thoughts, desires, and emotions. It's addressed as the center of your purposes and motivations. The author is saying, in Proverbs 4:23, This is what drives you, this is what controls you, this is what shapes your living. You have got to be concerned about the physical and spiritual condition of your heart. King Solomon, who wrote the Proverbs, was a man of great wisdom and was the wisest man who ever lived in his day. He got his wisdom through a dream encounter with God, who asked him what he wanted. Solomon's only request to God was to have wisdom to rule God's people well, (see 1 Kings 3:9). According to Proverbs 4:1, 20 Solomon is teaching his children about living a safe and godly life.

Another viewpoint is found in Deuteronomy. "Take heed to yourselves, lest your heart be deceived, and you turn aside and serve other gods and worship them,". According to Deuteronomy 11:16 NKJV, God is explaining to the Israelites that if they don't pay attention and live by the moral standards He has set for them, they will fall into the traps of the enemy. They will be deceived and led astray from Him and may not even know it. God tells us numerous times in the Bible that Satan, the enemy, is cunning and we must learn how to be aware of his tactics. But more than that, God teaches that our own heart does more damage to who we are than the enemy. He says to "take heed to yourselves, lest you be deceived". What is He warning us about? What does God want us to understand?

It seems that His message is that we are responsible for the condition or state our heart is in and we have the power to control it. But because the fallen nature of man has a propensity toward the things of this world rather than the things of God, we must utilize God's word as the measuring stick to determine what's godly and the road of life to travel. Since the wickedness of the human heart was inherited from the original act of sin, by Adam, there is no other way to set godly standards. This is also why Jesus says in Mark 7:20-22 NIV "What comes out of a person is what defiles them. For it is from within, out of a person's heart, that evil thoughts come sexual immorality, theft, murder, adultery, greed, malice, deceit, lewdness, envy, slander, arrogance, and folly."

God has empowered us through free will, to choose to be an evil-doer or do good or be godly. Notice that doing good is not the same as godly. In short, you can do good by anyone's standards, but you can only be godly by God's standards. During a time in my career as a Director of Nurses, one of my responsibilities was to ensure the staff were informed of and adhered to the policies and procedures developed to guide patient care and services. There were occasions when staff members decided not to follow those guidelines as written. They felt they had a better, more convenient way to perform the task assigned. When we don't follow standards and guidelines, someone will always suffer, the outcome will not be the quality expected, and there are consequences that must be endured.

But when we choose to go by our own decisions that don't line up with the instructions given, we set ourselves up for going astray and possible destruction. God is saying in Deuteronomy, that you don't have to be deceived if you stay the course I have set you on. The Lord reveals His love for us in Psalm 37:23-24, the Lord directs the steps of the godly. He delights in every detail of their lives. Though they stumble, they will never fall, for the Lord holds them by the hand.

I can recall times when I was in a very dark place mentally and emotionally, due to domestic violence. I was deceived about who I was as a person. I knew God, but I didn't have a relationship with Him through Christ at that time. I remember telling the few friends I had, that if I was not a "Mrs. Somebody, then I was nobody." My whole worth and value system was tied to being married from the age of 17.

From my heart, this is how I thought and what I believed. I had no self-identity unless I belonged to someone. Knowing about God didn't make me feel that I belonged to Him. I prayed and went to church every so often but I also learned how to play the part of "everything is fine". I had to hide the guilt, the shame, and the embarrassment of my situation. I had to learn to play the part for fear of someone seeing right through me and finding out what was really going on. I played it so well, that I deceived myself. In my heart, I felt like no one cared, but at the same time, I became a very good actress. During those times in my life, I never realized how bad off I really was. God through Christ has had to work overtime, chiseling away the junk I stuffed in my own heart over the years because of the long-term effects of abusive relationships. As I am sharing in this book, I dare not say He is finished. Oh, but I thank God for reaching out to a poor miserable person like me so many years ago.

As we continue talking about the heart and the many lessons we find in the Bible, let's briefly unpack Matthew 5:28 NKJV-"But I say to you that whoever looks at a woman to lust for her has already committed adultery with her in his heart." Jesus is teaching that before you commit an act of sin, it formulates as a thought in your heart first. Jesus goes beyond the outward command to reveal that the act is the result of an inner attitude of lust in the heart. He further distinguishes the ordinary glance from a "look to lust"

James 1:14-15 NIV sheds more light on that subject by explaining it like this, "but each person is tempted when they are dragged away by their own evil desire and enticed. Then, after desire has conceived, it gives birth to sin; and sin, when it is full-grown, gives birth to death."

Everyone will come up against temptations as long as we live, but it's not a sin to be tempted. Here James warns us of the consequence of giving in to our ungodly desire. When we say "yes" to the desire to do what we want, instead of trusting God and following His lead, sin is born. The desire has to have a decision, the decision of yes becomes action which produces the sin. James made it clear that temptation to sin always comes from within ourselves, the heart. It's never God's fault. No matter how terrible our circumstances are, the desire and follow through to sin is still ours. We choose to submit to the temptation of sin. Satan can only influence us by painting a picture for us to "look at" but he cannot make us choose to buy it. God provides trials and ordeals as a way to exercise and strengthen our faith according to 1 Peter 1:6-7.

Understanding God's word helps you to realize what's hot and happening in your heart; and what condition your heart is in. You will always live your life under the control and attitude of the heart. That means for lasting change to happen, it has to start with your heart. The word of God says the heart is the most important asset you have which is why it makes more sense to allow God to have control of it. It helps to remember that your greatest problem in all of life doesn't exist outside of you; it's not those less-than-perfect people and all those less-than-perfect places in your life. Your greatest problem is inside of you. It's the thoughts, motives, and idols of your own heart. You can't control the attitudes and actions of others, but you can control how they affect your life.

For years now, Proverbs 4:23 has been one of my power verses. A verse that God used to speak directly into specific situations and circumstances which caused a stirring in my heart so profoundly I couldn't ignore it, even during those times when I tried. As God was bringing about my healing process, He began to impress in my spirit that the issues of life really do relate to the condition of the heart. In other words, the state of our heart has significant influence in determining the matter and outcome of any given situation.

It determines how we respond or react when engaging others. It determines if our immediate surroundings are an environment of peace or chaos, joy or despair. It determines if we always point out the faults of others while assuring ourselves that we have none. Whatever is stored up in the heart will dictate what you say, what you look at, and where you go. A grieving or broken heart can become a bitter, hateful, and vengeful heart if left unchecked. A heart left unchecked may also become self -centered, self-absorbed, and self-obsessed. Our personalities, our intellects, and our moral states are products of what's in our hearts.

The condition of the heart impacts how we view society, each other, and ourselves. But more importantly, it determines how we view God which determines our relationship with Him. It reflects what we really believe about Him, what we believe about Jesus Christ, as Savior and Lord, and what we believe about the Holy Spirit and the Scriptures. Sin starts in the heart (see Matthew 15:19).[18]

Before sin becomes something we say or do, it must be a thought first. Since this is true, we do have a window of opportunity to counteract. Proverbs 4:23 KJV reads "Keep thy heart with all diligence; for out of it are the issues of life." The New International Version reads, "Above all else, guard your heart, for everything you do flows from it." The New Living Translation reads, "Guard your heart above all else, for it determines the course of your life." Being able to understand that the issues of life start with the thoughts and intentions of the heart, is a powerful tool to help navigate day-to-day experiences. Understanding and applying the word of God effectively can mean the difference between winning or losing your mental and emotional battles.

Part of the battle is recognizing who is in the battle. It will always be one of three persons in the battle with you—the Lord, yourself, or Satan, the original opponents in the garden. And for Christians, the truth be told, Satan spends more time influencing us to fight against God or ourselves, than battling him or his demons. The heart is the fountain from which the action springs.

If the fountain is pure, the action that flows from it will be pure. So one of the effective strategies to guard our heart includes a clean thought life. What does that mean? Simply put, you must be careful what you look at, listen to, where you go, and who you hang out with. If we measure everything by God's standards, just like we follow those policies and procedures to keep our jobs, we are protecting our hearts and giving our minds a chance to think clean thoughts.

In the Strong's Concordance #3820, the Hebrew word *leb* indicates one's emotions and understanding was centered in the heart, (see Proverbs 15:13-14). This concept blurs the dichotomy between mind and heart, intellect and emotions. So who determines that the heart or the mind is the foundation on which to build our mental, emotional, and spiritual well-being? Man or God? Let's take a look at what some of the greatest minds in human history have to say.

In the fourth century B.C.E., the Greek philosopher Aristotle (384-322 BCE) identified the heart as the most important organ of the body, the first to form according to his observations of chicken embryos. It was the seat of intelligence, motion, and sensation yet is also a hot, dry physical organ.[22] Through a series of experiments of dissecting animals, Aristotle concluded that the heart was the origin of veins in the body as well as the center of the psycho-physiological system. He also stated that the existence of pneumo (an ancient Greek word for "breath' or in a religious context 'spirit') was in the heart and functions as a messenger carrying blood to the body and produces sensation.[21]

According to the National Institute of Neurological Disorders and Stroke:

"The brain is the most complex part of the human body. This three-pound organ is the seat of intelligence, interpreter of the senses, initiator of body movement, and controller of behavior. Lying in its bony shell and washed by protective fluid, the brain is the source of all the qualities that define our humanity. The brain is the crown jewel of the human body."[20]

What does this mean from God's perspective? Before the fall of man, God saw everything He created was good. But after the fall, God identified the heart as the center of rebellion, producing disobedience and destruction (Genesis 8:21; Deut 6:5). To remedy this, God was determined to replace the "stony heart" with a "heart of flesh," one which would love, desire and follow Him (see Ezekiel 36:26-27). This process was already included in God's plan of redemption that would come to fruition at His appointed time. Our Lord really desires that we understand the human heart from His perspective in order to respond to Him and life appropriately and effectively. So let's examine some related Scriptures to obtain some divine knowledge and wisdom

Matthew 15:17-19 (NKJV)-[17] "Do you not yet understand that whatever enters the mouth goes into the stomach and is eliminated? [18]But those things which proceed out of the mouth come from the heart, and they defile a man. [19] For out of the heart proceed evil thoughts, murders, adulteries, fornications, thefts, false witness, blasphemies"

19th-Century British Pastor, author and theologian Charles Spurgeon speaks on the matter of Matthew 15:17-19-"It is not that which we eat that defiles us. If it is such food as we ought to take, it builds up the body. If it is improper food it may injure the body, yet it is not in itself capable of being regarded as sin; but a spiritual thing,—a thought, a desire, an imagination,—comes out of the heart, and if that is evil, it does defile the man. What a horrible den the heart itself must be, then! If all these evils come out of it, what a nest of unclean things it must be! A dreadful sight to the all-seeing God must be an uncleansed human heart. Let me read this verse again' "for out of the heart proceed evil thoughts, murders, adulteries, fornications, thefts, false witness, blasphemies. All these evils come out of the heart of man, out of such a heart as yours until it is renewed by grace. Though you sit very attentively in the house of God, unless his grace has changed your heart, all these evil things are there, and they only want an opportunity to come out and reveal themselves."[3]

Proverbs 4:23(KJV) -"Keep thy heart with all diligence; for out of it are the issues of life."

According to Matthew Henry's Concise Commentary—"There is in the word of God a proper remedy for all diseases of the soul. Keep thy heart with all diligence. We must set a strict guard upon our souls; keep our hearts from hurting and getting hurt. A good reason is given; because out of it are the issues of life. Above all we should seek from the Lord Jesus that living water, the sanctifying Spirit, issuing forth unto everlasting life. Thus we shall be enabled to put away a froward mouth and perverse lips; our eyes will be turned from beholding vanity, looking straight forward, and walking by the rules of God's word, treading in the steps of our Lord and Master.

Proverbs 23:7 (NKJV) -"For he is the kind of person who is always thinking about the cost. 'Eat and drink,' he says to you, but his heart is not with you."

This verse teaches that the man who says, "eat and drink" but is really begrudging the cost in his heart, is betraying his true feelings with his false words. He doesn't want you to eat his food and drink his wine at his expense. Additionally, some people do not say what they are thinking. For instance, this greedy man does not really want you to eat and drink what he has. So if you are invited to eat by this man, it would be best to decline because every bite must be considered and there will be a price to pay later.

What comes out of the heart reflects who we are. No matter how hard we try to hide it away, it will show up. It's easy to be graceful and kind when we are on the mountaintop and all is well. But when we fall and hit the valleys of life the darkness in our heart spews out. The heart is the fountain from which the action springs. If the fountain is pure, the action that flows from it will be pure.

Proverbs 21:2 NIV "A person may think their own ways are right, but the Lord weighs the heart."

You are to carefully weigh your heart at all times to ensure it remains pure. This calls for vigilance and allowing God to search your heart and show you if there is any evil in it. So we see that the heart is very important, both as a physical organ that pumps the blood for life throughout our physical body and as the source of spirit life. Nothing in our life deserves and requires more constant attention than our heart. Whatever is stored in the heart will dictate what we say, what we look at and where we choose to go. We must set a strict guard over our soul, keeping our hearts from hurting others and using practical application of the word of God when our heart gets hurt. A desire to hear, study and meditate on the word of God is a good sign that God's grace is working in our hearts.

God's word must be the absolute weapon of choice for Christians. The Apostle Paul explained to the Christians at Ephesus, that the full armor of God included the word of God which is the sword of the Spirit (see Ephesians 6:17). The power of God's grace is further revealed when godly fruit is produced as evidence of its work in progress. This fruit is not the works of the hands but rather works of the heart that produce moral purity of character. Then external fruit or works is the result of the purity of character.

Having knowledge and understanding is power. God made the human body so wonderful and profound, who can really know it but Him? And yet He gives us information and strategies to help us find our way and make decisions that guide our path in life. We may have to take medications to help improve our physical health and we may need the help of counselors or therapists for our mental and emotional well-being. But how can we heal as a whole person if we don't include treatment for our soul?

Lord God, my Father, I praise you and magnify Your Holy name for being our God. You are so kind, thoughtful and just. Thank you for giving us understanding and guidance so we can choose to live the life that You intended. I pray that You would sanctify me completely from my inner spirit to my outer actions, making my life stand out to others as an example of Your grace, Your love and Your mercy. In Jesus name, Amen.

CHAPTER FIVE

DO YOU WANT TO BE MADE WHOLE?

Our psychological makeup is developed and shaped by the myriad of experiences early in life. Any type of abuse at any age certainly has been proven to have a profound impact on the developing brain. That impact comes at a deep and lasting cost for the individual. Abuse and mistreatment are not something that we just "get over". Sometimes that may be easy for therapists or counselors to encourage someone to do and there may even be some effective steps to help minimize the outward display of a more subverted behavior. While the ultimate issue is how some people's hearts can be so filled with darkness that they can severely hurt, abuse, and mistreat others, those of us on the receiving end can take a stand against the long-term effects that can remain deeply seeded in our mental, emotional, and spiritual makeup.

It takes a great deal more than just learning to modify or control one's actions in response to the effects of these unnatural experiences. We must always strive for total deliverance from the profound strongholds of the enemy. We can fight against this widespread war of injustices and by God's grace, we have the power to experience holistic healing.

What is holistic healing? Holistic medicine is a form of healing that considers the whole person, body, mind, and spirit, in the quest for optimal health and wellness. According to the holistic medicine philosophy, one can achieve optimal health by gaining proper balance in all areas of the human makeup. [21]

Every part of a person's being must be considered in holistic healing to establish and maintain balance. To accomplish this, we must review resources from both a natural and spiritual perspective. The makeup of human beings is material and immaterial (body/soul/spirit) and each part must be treated respectfully. This diagram reflects the components of holistic care for which the intervention must be defined.

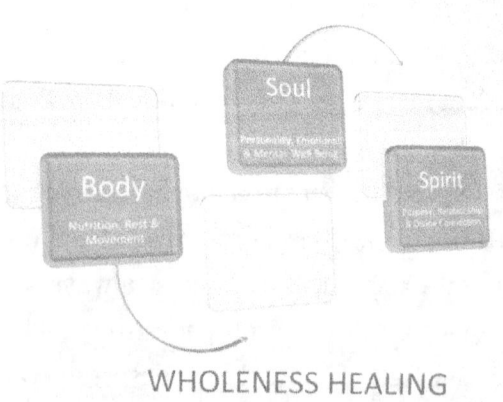

WHOLENESS HEALING

Interventions and Healing for the Physical Man

All symptoms that may be exhibited should be assessed, and diagnosed and treatment initiated as soon as possible. Timeliness is critical because symptoms of one illness or disorder can mask the presence of another. Listed are some outward displays seen on examination that could be the symptom of an underlying mental or emotional distress rather than a physical disorder. For example, a person could present with symptoms of a psychotic break, such as irrational or aggressive behavior, and yet an abnormally high blood sugar could be the problem. Research has proven that appropriate and timely diagnosis and treatment of unhealthy physical or mental symptoms can:

> Improve the chances of healing and well-being restoration.
> Lower the risk for other conditions and complications later in life.
> Reduce risky behaviors like smoking, and heavy drinking.
> Improve education and job potential.
> Reduce the risk of adverse experiences from being passed from one generation to the next.

Consider the physical body and its natural functions and abilities. It is amazing and unique from all other creations. When God designed it, He included the ability for it to heal and repair itself depending on the hurt. God stored an onsite pharmacy, open 24 hours a day, seven days a week, buried in the deep internal seams of our souls' garments.

When an infection attacks the body, the pharmacy automatically sends white blood cell soldiers to the front lines to deal with the intruders. When a bone is broken, the pharmacy dispatches special cells to the site. These cell warriors begin to form special protective blood clots and calluses around the break. This protective activity allows time for tiny, new threads of bone to form around the site and grow toward closing the fracture. When you get a cut, a scratch, or other skin injury, your blood is designed to form clots to stop the bleeding. While other working cells remove their dead, the injured and the new healthy cells work together to repair the damaged tissue. We further know that even the more critical organs with serious wounds have been known to heal and restore their normal functions. In my career as a registered nurse, I've witnessed cases of complete or partial recovery of the brain's abilities in numerous patients with significant injuries or illnesses. I have seen patients with severe dementia respond to nothing and no one except the preached word of God or gospel songs they once knew.

The design of the human body is amazing and unparalleled to any other even though it may need a little external help sometimes. Maybe it needs a little help with pain from illness to injury when you may need to take a few pills, add a few bandages, or give it a little therapy from time to time. No wonder King David says "I will praise you, for I am fearfully and wonderfully made; marvelous are thy works..." Psalm 139:14 KJV. So all physical functions are taken into consideration and magnified within the realm of holistic healing.

Understanding our Immaterial Makeup

Before we can really get into holistic healing, we must understand that the content of the immaterial part of man is both soul and spirit. These terms are often used interchangeably, however, from the perspective of our human makeup, they are very different. Both terms originate in the ancient Hebrew, Aramaic, and Greek languages. Holistic healing requires that the body, soul, and spirit of man be acknowledged and addressed in its appropriate context respectfully.

The Soul and Spirit

The primary use of the word soul, in Hebrew and Aramaic, "nephesh" (Strong's #5315) means "a breathing creature, the self, life or heart. To breathe, respire, be refreshed and the act of breathing". In Greek, the word soul is translated as "psuche" (Strong's #5590) and its primary meaning is "the vital source that animates the body and shows itself breathing. The seat of feelings, desires, affections and aversions". [27]

The first time the word soul is used in the Bible is in Genesis 2:7 (KJV), "And the LORD God formed man from the dust of the ground, and breathed into his nostrils the breath of life, and man became a living soul." This is a clear picture of the use of the word in its appropriate ancient language translations and primary meaning. This passage reflects both the creation of the material body from the physical matter of the literal earth and the immaterial component being given by God which produces animation in the physical matter.

Psychology is simply the study of the soul, from the Greek word *psuche*, "the immaterial part of man" which encompasses our mental and emotional state of being. The development of our personality is in this seat. Sigmond Freud uses the analogy of the Id, ego, and super-ego for structural models of the mind as the personality develops.

"Freud believed that events in our childhood have a great influence on our adult lives, shaping our personality. For example, anxiety originating from traumatic experiences in a person's past is hidden from consciousness and may cause problems during adulthood (in the form of neuroses)." [28]

According to Encyclopedia Britannica, Inc. the soul is "the spiritual part of a person that is believed to give life to the body and in many religions is believed to live forever... a person's deeply felt moral and emotional nature." [29]

The Merriam-Webster online dictionary says the soul is "the immaterial essence, animating principle, or actuating cause of an individual life; the spiritual principle embodied in human beings, all rational and spiritual beings, or the universe; the moral and emotional nature of a human being." [26]

The Hebrew and Aramaic word for spirit is *ruwach* (Strong"s #7307) and its primary use is "breath, air, wind, a breeze, air for breathing, the breath of one's mouth (as in speaking)". Psalms 33:6 (KJV) says "By the word of the LORD were the heavens made; and all the host of them by the breath of his mouth."

In Greek, the word for spirit is pneuma (Strong's #4151) and its primary use is the same as in Hebrew, breath, breeze, a current of air... It is clear that the wind in the Bible is regarded as a fitting emblem of the mighty penetrating power of the invisible God." [27]

The first reference to the Spirit in the KJV Bible is Genesis 1:2 revealing God's Spirit in the original creation of the heavens and the earth. The Bible never tells us that God is a soul or has a soul. According to John 4:24 (KJV), Jesus says that "God is a Spirit and they that worship Him must worship Him in spirit and truth."

Part of the significance of wisdom in understanding the difference between the soul and spirit is related to the healing processes we implement, activate, or benefit from. Our soul belongs to our human body to generate all fleshly responses to our surroundings, generate our emotions, and include our free will make up. God gives us a soul at the moment of conception which is when we become a living soul in a body. He gives us all the properties to develop a great personality to be shaped based on our choices and life experiences.

God desired for us to live, to love, to have wonderful human relationships and so much more. But because of one man's action (Adam), our soul became the unredeemed part of us that needed to be atoned for. Our spirit was the portion of the immaterial life that was given to us exclusively to connect us with our Creator. As God imparted His breath into the clay figure, His breath was the wind that gave us human life and the spirit was included to give us spiritual life.

The soul connects us to our worldly environment and our spirit life literally connects us in a spiritual relationship with the Godhead, (Holy Trinity). However, the fall of humanity in the garden resulted in complete spiritual separation from God which is called spiritual death. Holistic healing requires fixing this broken relationship.

2. *Interventions and Healing of the Psychological (mental & emotional) Man*

Mental trauma is one of the most common psychological health conditions in the world. What someone does to us is very impactful but how we perceive their actions is more significant and determines the level of devastation to our mental well-being. Mental and emotional healing is "the process of alleviating or attempting to alleviate mental or physical illness through the power of the mind, typically using such methods as visualization, suggestion, and the conscious manipulation of energy flow." [23]

The American Counseling Association (ACA) provides information on professional counselors around the world for just about anything you need. They also provide information on how to find a professional counselor for areas of life coaching, mentoring, marriage, psychological, financial well-being, and more. If you need it, you name it, you can find it, especially in the US. Resources also include support groups, hotlines, and outpatient organizations. I have included a list of hotline numbers by state in the US in the appendix of this book as well as other valuable resources. There are of course those inpatient facilities for those urgent situations. Evidence-based services and supports can promote protective factors that mitigate the effects of mistreatment as well as provide families and communities with the tools to stop it before it happens.

When Pastors or other spiritual leaders engage in counseling or coaching sessions with traumatized individuals, there may be times when specialized professional interventions are needed for effective treatment and healing. Prayerfully, those spiritual leaders will be able to recognize those needs and make proper referrals for the well-being of God's children. Spiritual leaders should also be more aware of techniques and instruments that are free and readily available for their use to enhance the counseling effectiveness. Choosing to use tools that have already been tried and tested with proven reliability and effectiveness will greatly improve the healing process for the person with whom they are working. These assessment tools are very successful in helping to guide counseling sessions towards identifying the underlying or root cause of a condition as well as being suggestive toward proper treatment. A few of those assessment tools available today are:

- Trauma-Informed Care Resource Guide by The Crisis Prevention Institute
- https:/www.thecenterofhope.org/wp-content/uploads/2019/10/Trauma-Informed-Care-Resources-Guide-CPI.pdf
- Environmental Influences on Child Health Childhood Trauma Questionnaire ECHO-wide Cohort Version 01.20 / November 30. 201823 https://www.henryford.com/-/media/files/henry-ford/hcp/research/hdrc/hdrc-questionnaires/ctq-

childhood-trauma-questionnaire-20181130-v01-20.pdf?
rev=fc73aee19e0e4012b1c9455af5474055&hash=B687508
0173CF13D298E9D6A3A9BC2CB
* CDC Adverse Childhood Experiences (ACE) Questionnaire:https://www.ncjfcj.org/wp-content/
uploads/2006/10/Finding-Your-Ace-Score.pdf

If we are really honest, it's almost impossible to go through childhood and adolescence without experiencing some sort of traumatic event. Obviously, the causes range from one extreme to the next. They go from punishment and ridicule to abuse and neglect. Some effects may even be subconsciously self-inflicted without an identified root cause. From the time we enter this cold and wicked world, severed from the warmth and protection of our mothers' womb we begin to experience what could be considered trauma such as: hunger, wet, hurting, desiring loving arms without being able to explain what's wrong with us, right? So the concept of healing impacts everyone and should be important for all, at least to some degree.

There are a myriad of resources available to assist in the healing processes of our mental and emotional conditions which include prescription medications, if warranted. But all these external treatment plans do us no good if we can't or won't admit we have a problem. If we allow society's stigmas, embarrassment, humiliation, and fear of vulnerability to keep us from being transparent with our issues, then we keep ourselves in bondage. We place strongholds in our own minds that prevent anyone or anything from penetrating the barrier; this may often include God.

So as the saying goes, the first step to healing is admitting you have a problem. But this must also include a desire to get to the bottom or identify the root cause, the real motivation of the mental or emotional condition. Sometimes it takes tracing symptoms of depression back to a point in time, event, or circumstance. Sometimes it really doesn't matter who did what, but rather your perception of who did what. It may be that over time, the psychological stronghold simply became a safe haven for your feelings and emotions. Maybe staying in isolation or keeping others at arm's length in relationships was a way to cope and avoid dealing with the effects of what happened so many years ago. Any one of these effects can become strongholds deep in our psychological makeup at a subconscious level. Even though these strongholds or bonds may have been created by some external force, we don't have to allow them to stay.

When we review some of the effects trauma has on our mental and emotional health, they are all related to our soul, our flesh, and our feelings. Some of the most common unhealthy conditions that people deal with are depression, anxiety, and fear. These lead to other unhealthy emotions like low self-esteem, lack of self-confidence, poor self-worth, and more. Some internal symptoms that I can identify with are exhibited under these unhealthy conditions:

- Talking negative or making light jokes about yourself
- Always blaming yourself when things go wrong
- Focusing on your negatives rather than positives
- Seeking others to give you worth and value in life
- No energy or desire to just take care of yourself
- Avoiding challenges for fear of failure
- Difficulty accepting compliments
- Poor sleep habits
- Malaise - general feelings of uneasiness or unrest with no identified cause
- Poor appetite and fatigue

There are also external displays of unhealthy mental or emotional conditions, which may present themselves in behaviors such as:

- Aggression towards others
- Poverty without seeking help
- Imprisonment due to acts of violence
- Self-harm, self-mutilation
- and much more

These outward displays are certainly more obvious to recognize and they are usually related to an internal disaster that has gone on too long and has erupted.

We are talking about the condition of our mind and soul and how we can improve its well-being. God gave it to us; that means we have the ability to control how healthy or unhealthy it is. This includes seeking as much help as we need to make it happen but never giving up.

Below are some strategies that I used to overcome the effects of traumatic events that occurred in my early life:

Using pen and paper is a must: Putting things on paper always helped me to get negative and confusing thoughts out of my head. Once I could see them, I would think through what might really be going on. When people beat up on you physically, mentally, or emotionally, it will usually impact your personality in one of two ways. Either you internalize the effects or you project them externally through behavior and attitude.

Some examples of trauma effects caused me to internalize and self-isolate. I refused to let others completely into my heart. Physically, you would never know it because I could always function in any given situation, but I didn't let anyone get too close. I always had trouble developing deep relationships to the point of instinctively pushing people away if I felt they were getting too close. Subconsciously, I guess that was also a protective mode, at least that's what the enemy made me think until the Light of God shined on it and showed me the truth.

Rev. Dr. Marilyn McClain

Not only was I keeping others out of my heart, I was keeping Him out as well, or rather not allowing Him to do His work of healing. Understand that even at this time, I was a saved, born-again Christian, but my walk with God was hindered by all this darkness. As I was led to write these feelings and thoughts down, I could see, literally, that God was revealing to me some of the problems and the root causes. Then I would pray about them and make conscious, intentional efforts to think differently about them.

Yes, we must guard our hearts as the Scripture tells us in Proverbs 4:23, from all evil, but not by being isolated from intimate relationships. Instead, we guard it by filling it with divine truths from God's word and living by those truths. We guard it by:

- Filling it with the love, peace and joy of an intimate relationship with our Savior and Lord
- Filling it with the Holy Spirit to allow His power to change how we think, how we respond to our situation and circumstances, and how we allow the impact of other people's actions to affect us.
- Filling it with the truths in the word of God

When I changed how I saw my issues, the effects they had on me began to change. Many times it took getting the problem on paper to see it more clearly.

Work on changing things you can change: Make a note of a specific issue and its outcome for later review. This is very encouraging to look back on and see any progress made or not made. It was beneficial for me because my journaling became a witness to myself. I was testifying to myself in writing with dates, times, and outcomes as to what the Lord was doing, and how He was moving in my life just because He could and just because He loved me for no reason.

So when I would look back and review my writings, I was so impressed with God's input, it was invigorating. Too often I saw my problems bigger than God which caused me to believe they would never change. But the more God reminded me that "..greater is He that is in me, than he that is in the world, I John 4:4, I learned nothing is impossible with God. I let God do the work and I got the benefits. Yes, I said "let Him" because He will not override our freedom Of choice.

For the activity of God's power to be most effective in our day-to-day lives, we have to choose to allow His convictions and conversions. Although evil is real, we have the promise that the one who is in us is greater than the one who is in the world (1 John 4:4). Jesus saves us, trains us to resist the power of evil, and delivers us from anything that holds us back. With Jesus, we can be truly made whole and free forever.

Volunteer to help others: Helping others often makes you feel better about your self-worth. Getting involved with the needs of others with no ulterior motives certainly was therapeutic for me. I would volunteer to help people move furniture, grocery shop, or other tasks. I would even provide spiritual, and other types of counseling; anything I could do to help someone else gave me a mental break.

It didn't make my problems go away, but it did reduce the time I spent stressing over issues, trying to figure it out. When helping others led me to get a good physical workout-such as helping people move furniture, my added benefit was a great night of restful sleep.

Watch who you hang with: Try to avoid hanging out with people who always tell you what you can't do or how bad you are, even when it's family. Sometimes you have to love them from a distance. The Bible states in Psalm 1:1 (NKJV), "Blessed is the man who walks not in the counsel of the ungodly, nor stand in the path of sinners, nor sit in the seat of the scornful;" which means to avoid those with evil influence, those that do evil deeds and have evil thoughts. Avoid toxic relationships. Stay clear of those whose feet always run toward violence or immorality.

Refuse to allow others to draw you into negative and vile conversations. Psalm 1:1 also teaches us that there is a process to our actions for good or evil. If you walk toward it to be nosy, you can get drawn in. You will know that you're getting drawn in when you stand and listen too long because what you hear or see becomes interesting. Before you know it, you get comfortable and take a seat to stay a while. Now, your light has grown dim because you allowed too much darkness to enter. I never really had a lot of people I just hung out with, even in my youth, so this was not much of a problem for me in that sense.

Mine was worse, I think, and I couldn't get away from her (ME). I have always been my own worst enemy. I beat myself up so much more than anyone else could. I didn't need any help. I kept myself from opening up to others, I wouldn't let people get too close. I tried to make sure they only saw a well-functioning person on the outside rather than the despairing person on the inside.

Maybe I was afraid of what they might think of me if they knew the real me. Maybe I was afraid of seeing the real me, myself, and maybe a bit of both because I didn't know what to do with that person. Trust me, when you don't talk to people, you will talk to yourself and usually those conversations are damaging and condemning. But oh, how I thank God for always stepping in even when I didn't ask Him. Realizing He had been trying to talk to me and get me to listen to Him all along, I now had a True Friend to hang out with.

Don't let perceptions dictate your response: One of the greatest accomplishments during my time of healing was not to allow the perception of my external situation and circumstances to dictate my mental and emotional response to them. The Lord taught me how to look at the internal motivation of the effects of the issue rather than the external reason. I learned to determine and define the effects an issue had on me, regardless of the situation or who was involved. No one and nothing has the right to have that much power over me but me and God. He reminded me of His word in 2 Corinthians 10:4-5, that anything, any thought, any action, or any person that exalted itself above the truth and the knowledge of God is of the enemy and therefore is a lie from the pit of hell. Those things must be brought into captivity to the obedience of Christ in order for the stronghold to be broken.

Understanding and applying this truth and concept helped me take back my joy from the symptoms of depression. It gave me the strength to refuse and live without the prescription medications my physician said I needed so many years ago. It helped me to see my depression was a result of trying to manage situations over which I had no control. Instead, it revealed that I had absolute control over how it made me feel, and therefore, I could control how I responded to those effects.

This came only by my trusting God, His grace, and His guidance in His word of truth. When I think about the goodness of God and how it shows up and goes to work actively on my behalf, my soul rejoices, I get so excited that I can run in celebration even when I'm all by myself. God helped me to see myself differently, to see the literal power He gave me to yield, to see me how He sees me. Then I saw my stuff, my situations, and circumstances that had me under its control differently, and I began to respond differently. I learned to respond in the person who is more than a conqueror that God created me to be.

When I learned who the real enemy of my soul was, then I learned how to fight using the ammunition God gave me-His Spirit and His word. But for it to be truly effective, I had to trust and believe in that ammunition. Before then I had it but didn't trust to use it, so I made it useless against my stuff. I truly learned what it means to say that this war is not carnal, not based on flesh and blood but spiritual, and thus, it is a spiritual fight, in need of spiritual weapons. However, everyone—body, soul, and spirit, has to come to the battle zone and do their part.

Do something relaxing: Before bedtime, drink a hot beverage, read a good book, or listen to soothing music. Since I'm a night owl, I didn't really do any of these things. But I've always been a workaholic with several projects going at the same time. For me, multitasking with several huge assignments was comfortable. I also perform well under pressure, even procrastinating until the last minute to get tasks completed.

However, God taught me that this behavior was actually a coping mechanism that kept me from dealing with some mental or emotional issues which included marriage and other relationship concerns. Being a workaholic allowed me to focus on work duties and responsibilities which kept me from dealing with the more important matters of home life. I guess I was trying to wish or work them away which obviously never worked. When God tries to get me to look at me so He can help me, sometimes it hurts, and it's scary. Many times it looked and felt so bad, I often attributed it to the devil's work, so I would just avoid dealing with it. I thought avoiding it was submitting it to God.

Oh was I wrong. The devil had me believing his lie which hindered my deliverance. But it was actually God trying to help and intervene His way. God will always do things His way because He knows His way is better for us. Needless to say, while I no longer fall prey to this behavior as a coping strategy, I still multitask but make adjustments and better decisions when needed.

• **Look in the mirror: Learn to love who's looking back at you the way God loves you**. Looking in the mirror was always a challenge for me. I seldom looked at myself because gushing over my looks, hair, make-up, and clothes was a waste of time. However, God revealed that I didn't like looking in the mirror because I really didn't like who was looking back. For me, avoiding the mirror was motivated by a deeper, darker pain that was tied to things that happened to me at an early age compounded by the effects of two abusive marriages.

When I was ready to listen, God helped me to see that avoiding the mirror was intentional. It was tied to my low self-esteem, low self-worth, and low self-confidence, all due to the long-term effects of trauma.

I actually felt insignificant, a product of the despair I had to keep hidden from the outside. I had to always appear to be okay on the outside when I was not okay on the inside. The despair and hopelessness were something only I saw, but there were times when I wondered if others could see through the mask. The lasting effects of trauma in my life impacted me in so many different ways, sometimes it was hard to even identify it. Without God, I'm sure much of this would not have come to light because I would not have allowed it to.

From 1988 until 1999, I owned and operated a Medicare-certified home health and hospice agency that only the Lord could have made possible. The Lord guided me through all the steps of obtaining the licenses and Certificate of Need (CON), required by law for this type of business. As God prospered the business, He opened some very influential doors that would help continue that prosperity. However, because of how I saw myself, low self-confidence, etc., I developed a literal fear of walking through those doors. I was afraid I would not be able to interact or compete at the level God was taking me. That fear showed itself in the inadequate business part of the operation rather than to the clinical side. While I was a good clinical manager, I prevented myself from being the businesswoman I thought I was. I prevented myself from going where God was trying to take me. So the motivation for avoiding the mirror ran much deeper than I could have imagined.

Since I have gotten older, wiser, and more knowledgeable through life's experiences with God and man, the long-term effects of abusive situations have become easier to identify. Now, at times, I look for them. I weigh negative, unhealthy thoughts, attitudes, or imagery in my mind against the truth of who I am in Christ Jesus and against His Truth, His word. Then if God gives me instruction or a challenge, *most of the time* I push through it no matter what I think the outcome may be. I leave the outcome to God.

While in seminary (2003-2006), students were given homework activities. We were to practice sermon presentations in a mirror and record it or watch one of our own actual sermon deliveries to evaluate areas of needed improvement. Well, needless to say, I was glad this activity was not for a grade. While other students discussed their detailed thoughts in class, I simply shared that it was a struggle for me because I thought I looked and sounded ridiculous and didn't feel I could benefit from that practice. Even today that's just not something I choose to do.

However, while writing this section of the book, God shows some of His humor in His presence. He uses a friend to send me a message that I thought was hilarious. It was a challenge to take time before finishing this section of the manuscript, pull a recorded worship service, watch, and listen to myself. That was it. I thought, *Really God! Why now?*

Even though I don't make special efforts to check myself in the mirror, I know who I am in Christ and I am comfortable and confident in that. But I did it because God sent the message. Wow, am I glad I did. I so enjoyed the sermon as I saw the powerful delivery by the presence of the Holy Spirit. It excited me all the more. I was sharing that test sent by God with a few other people, who rejoiced with me.

I was so glad to experience this and see how God continues to work on my behalf when I didn't even know I needed Him too in this area. God wanted me to see and understand that it's okay to look at myself and watch me do what I do, because it's no longer me that I'm looking at, but rather the Christ in me. Glory Hallelujah!

I'm so glad that God is not a magician who just pulls whatever we need or desire out of a hat and sends us on our way. But He is a God that desires we experience Him, His presence, and "all His benefits" Psalm 103:2 KJV. God uses every test, challenge, situation, and circumstance, no matter how great or small, to heal, deliver, and to grow us spiritually as we walk with Him. He shows us ourselves, to make us better than we could ever be on our own. God rarely fixes us immediately. Instead, He uses time factors, processes, and people to ensure permanent, long-lasting healing, deliverance, and restoration.

God explained to me in His word and proved to me in His Son that I was more valuable to Him than anyone in the world. He had a place for me in His heart and in His family regardless of who I was or was not. When that resonated in my soul and spirit, my life changed. By the grace of God, I love who I am now, where I am, and who God has created me to be. But there are still times when I have to make concerted efforts to look at myself in the mirror just to enjoy who's looking back. *Just being real!*

3. Interventions and Healing of the Social Man

There are numerous forms and methods used in the psychosocial healing process. Let's first understand what is social psychology. According to Merriam-Webster social psychology is "the study of the manner in which the personality, attitudes, motivations, and behavior of the individual influence and are influenced by social groups." [26]

"Aristotle believed that humans were naturally sociable, a necessity which allows us to live together (an individual-centered approach), whilst Plato felt that the state controlled the individual and encouraged social responsibility through social context (a socio-centered approach)." [31]

The American Psychological Association says, "Social psychologists are interested in all aspects of personality and social interaction, exploring the influence of interpersonal and group relationships on human behavior. The way we perceive ourselves in relation to the rest of the world influences our behaviors and our beliefs. The opinions of others also affect our behavior and how we view ourselves. Social psychologists are interested in all aspects of interpersonal relationships and the ways that psychology can improve those interactions. For example, their research helps us understand how people form attitudes toward others and, when these are harmful—as in the case of prejudice, for example—provides insight into ways to change them."[30]

All around us, we see family members consoling children and relatives, neighbors and peers sharing worries and losses, religious leaders caring for members of their communities, and mental health specialists or nonspecialists treating their clients. These are all significant relational processes required for social healing. Appendix D of this book has a "social wellness checklist" that was developed and made available by the National Institutes of Health (NIH). It includes how to develop positive social habits, tips on connecting with others, and guidance on 1 building effective support systems. You can access this tool on their website. https://www.nih.gov/health-information/social-wellness-toolkit

As we review and understand the various aspects of social healing, it is clear people make up a society. So regardless to the cultural or ethnic frame, socioeconomic status or other relational dynamics, the people in the society must have or strive to have a quality of life in their own physical, mental, emotional and spiritual well-being to propagate a healthy society.

I can recall one of my areas of social challenge was when I understood I had a people-pleasing problem. I would do, attempt to do, or agree to do almost anything someone asked of me just to please them, regardless of the impact it had on my life. Sometimes, it was not always someone asking, it was just me volunteering, in the heat of a moment and later wishing I had not, because I had absolutely no way of getting it done without compromising somewhere else.

Then I would get so frustrated trying to do what I said I would. It caused me tension, stress, muscle aches, and headaches which I internalized and it probably contributed to my being a workaholic as well. There were a few times where being a people pleaser caused me to lash out at others unintentionally but of course, I would apologize. Thank God He is always with us. The Lord taught me doing good for others is a great thing, but not at the expense of pleasing them at any cost and having to suffer the consequences. Those consequences may manifest physically, mentally or emotionally.

While the things I did were good and helpful or pleasing to others, God taught me that the motive for which I was doing them, was not of Him. It was a self-centered desire to please others at any cost and the cost was too high. Colossians 3 and Ephesians 6 both give guidance on how to avoid being a people pleaser. I learned to say "I'm sorry I can't." "Maybe another time," or "if you had told me earlier...", etc.

Hear me, reader. It's not enough to learn to respond in this manner, but God helped me to be okay with saying No. However, saying "No" brought about emotions of guilt and self-condemnation. In addition to these feelings of guilt when I said I can't, the guilt was compounded by a fear of disappointing someone, or what my no may have cost someone else, or what kind of bind I put others in.

Another aspect of being a people pleaser is that I was more concerned with what others thought or if they liked me, rather than what God thought about me. All of this and more weighs heavily on the mind of a people pleaser. These emotions are not just turned off or cast aside, once I ask God for help. They must still be dealt with to overcome and I had to start somewhere.

That meant first I had to recognize I had a people-pleasing problem and I was tired of falling into the enemy's trap. Well, as the saying goes, "be careful what you ask for because God will send tests your way. Tests that are specifically designed to help you overcome your issue and be delivered, but it may not always be pretty or painless. He will continue to send them until you begin to trust the guidance He is trying to give you.

By the way, that trust is also called faith. After various and numerous tests with people I cared about or some assignments on the job, I learned saying, "I can't, I'm sorry" was really okay. For my feelings of disappointing others, or fearful of what they thought, I learned to explain more of why I couldn't and was very apologetic if it inconvenienced anyone. If there were financial costs involved, I offered to help cover it, if I could. I still have a heart for helping others in any way I can, but I simply allow God to take the lead on the what, the how and the when *most of the time.*

It's also easier now to discern hearing God's voice versus following my own. Let me give you an example. In January 2023, a friend asked for my help as a nursing consultant. Immediately, I agreed. Then a month later they asked for a great deal more than I wanted to give. I prayed about it and God clearly said to only do what I originally agreed to do. They were in such a grave situation and I knew I could help. My heart went out to them, so I agreed to go the extra mile— much more than what God told me to do. I made a conscious decision to help a friend realizing I was choosing the people's need over God's instructions. Also, I realized I would endure whatever consequences that came, and I have regretted it ever since.

Trust me, reader, disobedience is a sinful act. Even if your intentions are pure, disobedience still hinders your closeness and fellowship with the Father. The consequences will always be worse than you can imagine. Don't do it! But let me clarify, it does not cause you to lose your position of salvation. I've learned firsthand that "sin will take you farther than you want to go, keep you longer than you want to stay and cost you more than you are willing to pay" is a true statement.

Even though God is faithful, He never left me and He brought some good out of my disobedience for my friend. My intimate closeness with Him was hindered for those six months and again I have regret. Of course, He's forgiven me and helped me forgive myself. That being said, once again, I am back on track as I follow His lead, praise You Lord! Oh, how awesome is my God!

God does not just remove our areas of imperfections or heal us from our unhealthy states, even though He can. If He did that then no one would ever experience convictions, conversions and transformation. It all has to develop through processes, through levels of acceptance and growth to be more beneficial, but God is always with us every step of the way. The best reason is that no one would ever get to actually know God and experience all that He is if He were just a spiritual vending machine. God's healing is always holistic when we ask and accept it His way. That's why Jesus always asked, "Do you want to be made whole?"

4. Interventions and Healing of the Spirit Man

a. The Sickness

As with the physical and psychological components of the human make-up, before moving into a discussion of healing, we must first understand more about the spirit component and what makes it sick.

It was explained earlier in this chapter, our spirit was given to keep us always pointed toward and connected to God, moving and existing exclusively for a relationship and fellowship with Him. God has always, before the foundation of the world, desired to dwell with His people. His plan has always been to bring His kingdom to earth so that He would be our God and we would be His people in His kingdom. In the study and insight of several Scriptures, God makes clear His desire to live among and dwell with His people. Here are a few for review:

- **Exodus 25:8 (NIV)** "Then have them make a sanctuary for me, and I will dwell among them.

- **1 Kings 6:13 (NKJV)** -"And I will dwell among the children of Israel, and will not forsake My people Israel."

- **Matthew 1:23 (NKJV)**-"Behold, the virgin shall be with child, and bear a Son, and they shall call His name Immanuel," which is translated, "God with us."

- **John 1:14 NKJV**-"And the Word became flesh and dwelt among us, and we have seen his glory, glory as of the only Son from the Father, full of grace and truth."

- 1 **Corinthians 6:19-20 (NKJV),** "Or do you not know that your body is the temple of the Holy Spirit who is in you, whom you have from God, and you are not your own? 20 For you were bought at a price; therefore glorify God in your body [a]and in your spirit, which are God's." [1]

- **2 Corinthians 6:16 (NKJV),** "And what agreement has the temple of God with idols? For you all are the temple of the living God. As God has said: 'I will dwell in them, And walk among them. I will be their God, And they shall be My people."

God provided a way and a place for His people to always be with Him, to draw near to Him and that has never changed. When that connection is not present our spirit yearns for relief. It seeks other ways to satisfy its appetites. It struggles to find its own way to hope, joy, peace, and love. Without that spiritual connection, the wholeness of a person is impaired desiring to be made whole. Unfortunately, mankind, in general, has not accepted the inspired written word of God as absolute truth. As a result, most seek to fulfill this spiritual deprivation in so many other ways. Therefore the spirit of man is sick, with a diagnosis of what I would call, "*spiritual separation syndrome*".

As a result of this spiritual separation syndrome, our soul makes choices to rebel against God and everything godly. It chooses to revel in self-centeredness, being self-absorbed thinking that we know what's best rather than God. When Adam decided to choose the fruit he saw with his natural eye, he chose human reasoning over divine intellect.

Our soul is made up of our emotions and mental capacities which are driven according to the needs and desires of the flesh. Since the spirit is separated from God, the soul alone does not desire a relationship with God nor follow the things of God. The soul of man is really not interested in who God is, what God wants or what God has to say. According to Romans 8:6-8 (NKJV), the soul of man is an enemy against God.

"[6]For to be carnally minded is death, but to be spiritually minded is life and peace. [7]Because the carnal mind is enmity against God; for it is not subject to the law of God, nor indeed can be. [8]So then, those who are in the flesh cannot please God".

The Strong Concordance #4559 Greek word for carnal is "sarkikos" and its primary use is pertaining to the flesh; temporal, animal, and unregenerate. So here in Romans, Paul wants us to understand that when the spirit is sick and not connected to the Father of it, then that person is controlled by the sensual, animal instincts and appetites of the flesh, just like any other animal. That person is governed by the human nature rather than the Spirit of God. Without the spiritual connection to God, we cannot please God or be in a relationship with God, no matter how hard we try. We see this truth explained here and restated in so many other passages of Old and New Testament Scriptures, such as Hebrews 11:6, (NIV): "And without faith it is impossible to please God, because anyone who comes to him must believe that he exists and that he rewards those who earnestly seek him."

Because the first Adam made the choice to go his own way and do his own thing, rather than trust and follow what God said, it cost everyone their spiritual connection with God. God said He created everything after it's kind. Not one species evolved into another species, but rather as each species mated they produced offspring of their own kind. This was the same with Adam and Eve.

As they mated, they passed to every offspring the human faulty nature or soul whose spirit is disconnected from God. As in Genesis 2:17 (KJV) "But you must not eat from the tree of the knowledge of good and evil, for when you eat of it you will surely die." God clearly gave them the heads up of what would happen if they ate from that tree, and they did it anyway. Since physical death did not happen immediately, Adam and Eve may have thought they were in the clear. However, they may not have understood that what God said was absolute truth and will come to pass, surely, they understood obedience. They made a choice to trust a lie rather than the truth. Basically, God said don't do it, or there will be consequences that you don't want to have to endure, but Satan said, do it because the consequences may not be as bad as what God said, (see Genesis 3:4-5).

The physical death of all creation did begin that fatal day in the garden but at a slow pace of decay. Paul tells us in Romans 8:22 (NKJV), "We know that the whole creation has been groaning as in the pains of childbirth right up to the present time." Creation was subjected to frustration, not by its own choice, but by the will of the one who subjected it. All of creation lives in the hope that it will be liberated from its bondage in death and decay one day by the glory of God. On that fatal day, God spoke absolute truth to Adam and Eve, "you will surely die..." which was an emphatic statement of absolute and immediate action. The immediate result was the spirit of man being disconnected from the Spirit of God. But we also see a much slower death through the deterioration of all creation.

There is no spiritual life without being connected to the Spirit Father. Every human being is born after Adam's kind, and therefore, inherits the spiritual disconnect from the Spirit Father. Hence, every human being is sentenced at conception with the terminal sickness of being born spiritually dead. However, there is One Cure. But first let's review some of the symptoms of an unhealthy spirit, one that is separated from the Father.

b. The Symptoms

Merriam-Webster defines the term "symptom" as "subjective evidence of disease or physical disturbances. something that indicates the existence of something else."

According to https://www.Britannica.com/dictionary a symptom is "a change in the body or mind which indicates that a disease is present... a change which shows that something bad exists",

This condition that I call "spiritual separation syndrome" is like a child that becomes separated from their loving parent. The child will experience symptoms of stress, anxiousness, fear, nightmares, coping issues and more. If this separation persists for a long period of time, their mental and emotional well-being will be affected and usually develop unhealthy and hazardous practices in life.

The Bible gives us examples of what the attitude, thoughts and behaviors of an unsaved or spiritually dead person look like in the passages below:

- **Genesis 8:21 (NKJV)**-"Then the Lord said in His heart, "I will never again curse the ground for man's sake, although the imagination of man's heart is evil from his youth…"". God says man's heart is still wicked. But what does society/the world say— humans believe the heart is inherently good. So in other words God must be a liar, right?
- **Hosea 8:4 (NIV)**-"They set up kings without my consent; they choose princes without My (God's) approval. With their silver and gold they make idols for themselves to their own destruction."
- **Matthew 15:19-21**-evil desires come from an evil heart. According to Strong's Concordance Hebrew #7451, 7563 and Gr. #2556, #4190, the primary use of the word "evil" is worthless, morally wrong, bad ungodly person, the devil or sinner. Bad character, bad disposition, being in the wrong, wicked and guilty enough to deserve punishment.
- **Psalm 68:1**-they are haters of the God of Scripture, and have no interest in or desire for God or the things of God.

- **2 Timothy 3:2** -They love themselves, they are lovers of money, boasters, proud, blasphemers, disobedient to parents, unthankful, unholy.

- **Proverbs 16:18** -their prideful heart leads them to destruction, just like Satan, they make themselves their god, they are selfish and self centered

- **1 Timothy 6:10** -they love money not realizing that loving it so much is the root of all evil, they never have enough, will do whatever it takes to keep getting more

- **Galatians 5:19-21-**they enjoy living by the works of the flesh, adultery, fornication, idolatry, hatred, contentions, selfish ambitions, jealousies, wrath,

- **Mark 10:17-31-**reject Jesus as Savior and Lord. Being just like the rich young ruler who decided his wealth was more important than what Jesus was offering

These symptoms or behaviors characterize the heart and soul of the unbeliever in that they practice and enjoy living in these sinful states without remorse and with no regard for the God of the Bible. However, it is important to note that Christians are also prone to live by the flesh acting like unsaved people, even though our spirit has made peace with God by grace through faith in Jesus Christ. 1 Corinthians 3:3(NLV) says, "You still live as men who are not Christians. When you are jealous and fight with each other, you are still living in sin and acting like sinful men in the world."

We also see how Paul himself struggled with the war of two members inside himself, in Romans 7, but then he gives credit and honor to Jesus for strength to fight against the flesh. Romans 7:19-20, 24-25 (NIV) says, "For I do not do the good I want to do, but the evil I do not want to do this I keep on doing. 20 Now if I do what I do not want to do, it is no longer I who do it, but it is sin living in me that does it... [24]O wretched man that I am! Who will deliver me from this body of death? [25]I thank God—through Jesus Christ our Lord! So then, with the mind I myself serve the law of God, but with the flesh the law of sin."

The difference between believers and non-believers is that believers should not love sin whereas non-believers love and enjoy indulging in sin. I know I did when I was in the world. Another difference is that the Holy Spirit indwells every believer. Thus being so, He gives us the power to choose to accept His work of convicting, converting and transforming those ungodly, unholy character flaws daily.

c. The Interventions:

Weapons of War

This battle of life is a spiritual battle and there is no way to fight a spiritual war with carnal weapons. This is a battle you are in whether you choose to be or not. Dear

Adam made that choice for all of us. Ultimately the battles rage because our real enemy is Satan who hates God and God's people. The persistent skirmishes, conflicts, and confrontations will rage on in this lifetime. The wickedness of the world, dark powers in high places, seated evil on the thrones of men will get even worse until God the Father and our Savior and Lord, Jesus Christ puts a final end to it and brings His kingdom to this place in its fullness. Glory, what a time that will be! Even though Jesus won the war and defeated the power of sin at the cross of Calvary and God sealed it with His Resurrection, the devil and evil influencing powers still tries to steal, kill and destroy our soul and spirit daily. Jesus says in John 10:10 NKJV, "The thief does not come except to steal, and to kill, and to destroy. I have come that they may have life, and that they may have it more abundantly." Anything and anyone who tries to steal, kill, or destroy our faith and trust in God is a thief.

Another reference is when Jesus informed Peter that Satan wanted to sift him like wheat, but Jesus said He prayed for him that his faith would not fail, see Luke 22:31-32. This was not just for Peter and his boys, but for all saints as members in the Body of Christ who would come after them. Satan wants to sift us all. Jesus gives life in its fullness and it is the epitome of holistic healing as only He can do. As Jesus died, believers are filled by Him with all spiritual blessings we need, lacking nothing, we are completed in Him (Colossians 2:10).

Having a relationship with Jesus is our greatest and most effective weapon for which He also provides the ammunition, His Word, by the power of the Holy Spirit.

There are thousands of resources for healing, hundreds of self-help books and programs, and thousands of licensed and certified counselors and clinicians that God has blessed to be available and capable of assisting with all the profound effects of trauma. But without the Person and Work of Jesus Christ atoning for the sins of the world and removing the power evil has in the world, the ultimate war could not be won. Being made whole could never take place without Jesus because there would be no True Light, no True Love, and no True spiritual life that could make a difference in real darkness. There would never have been a reconciliation of the spirit of man with the Spirit Father to avert the spiritual death.

Holistic healing has to begin with the framework of faith in the Living God and Jesus Christ, as Savior and Lord. Saving faith, a weapon that must be rooted and grounded in the virgin birth, the death on the cross, the resurrection of Jesus, and His purpose as sent by God. There can be no armor for battle without the weapon of faith. Ephesians 6:16 (NKJV) says "above all, taking the shield of faith with which you will be able to quench all the fiery darts of the wicked one." If God is so compassionate and loving to tell us there are battles we must fight, and then gives us the tools to win, why don't we use them? Only a foolish person would say, "no thanks, I'll fight my own way."

"For though we live in the world, we do not wage war as the world does. The weapons we fight with are not the weapons of the world. On the contrary, they have divine power to demolish strongholds. We demolish arguments and every pretension that sets itself up against the knowledge of God, and we take captive every thought to make it obedient to Christ," (2 Corinthians 10:3-5 NIV). Apostle Paul explains that a stronghold is a "mental block" that blocks our mind against the knowledge and understanding of God, His character, His nature, and His word. That mental block can be a belief in world systems or an attitude. That mental block also creates mental and emotional illnesses, such as fear, guilt, resentment, insecurity, and shame. Strongholds by the enemy keep unbelievers blinded, deaf, and dumb from receiving wisdom, knowledge, and understanding from God and His truths. They hinder and prevent unbelievers from coming to the Light of Jesus and receiving Him as Savior and Lord. If you never recognize it, you will never allow Jesus to make you free and make you whole.

Understanding What You Believe is Required

A study conducted in 2017 by the PEW Research Center reports that in recent years there has been a huge decline in the percentage of adult Americans who do not affiliate with a religious group. In spite of this trend, the majority of Americans say they believe in a god or a higher power, including agnostics and atheists. However, during this same study, only a small majority of adult Americans actually believe in the God of the Bible. The research report on this very specific question is reflected in the diagram. [32]

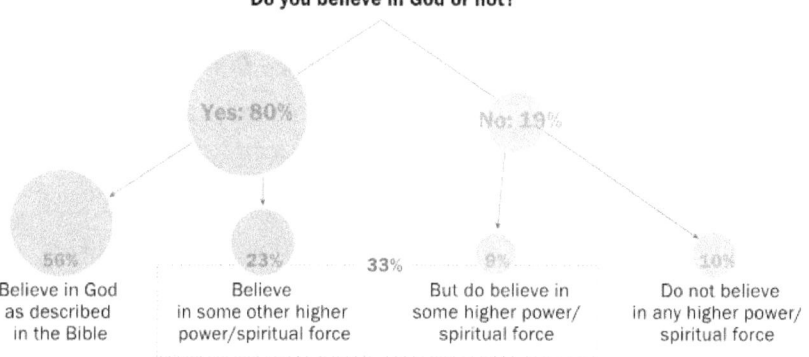

One-third of U.S. adults believe in a higher power of some kind, but not in God as described in Bible

Do you believe in God or not?

Yes: 80%   No: 19%

| 56% | 23% | 33% | 9% | 10% |
| Believe in God as described in the Bible | Believe in some other higher power/spiritual force | But do believe in some higher power/ spiritual force | Do not believe in any higher power/ spiritual force |

Note: Don't know or unclear responses not shown. Figures may not add to subtotals indicated due to rounding.
Source: Survey conducted Dec. 4-18, 2017, among U.S. adults.
"When Americans Say They Believe in God, What Do They Mean?"

PEW RESEARCH CENTER

When you go to the doctor and you are diagnosed with high blood pressure, they will first examine your symptoms trying to determine the root cause of the problem. There are different types of hypertension: essential, secondary, isolated systolic, malignant and benign. Once the physician feels they have established the cause, they will start you on a medication designed for that root cause. A few months down the road, that medication proves ineffective in getting your blood pressure under control. Then your symptoms of high blood pressure are still a problem, so the doctor prescribes something different. This cycle is continued until your symptoms of high blood pressure are under control with the right medication. The same principle is true as it relates to a sick spirit separated from God. People will try many things to fix the struggles of the spirit, but every intervention attempted will prove futile because there is only one Cure.

Being Open to Explore the God of the Bible is Required

The first and most important intervention for spiritual healing is to examine our faith. What is faith? Do I believe in the God of the Bible or not? Can I have faith without religion? Can I be a Christian without Christ? Will I go to heaven when I die because I'm a good person who does good things? Can I be spiritual and be spiritually dead? Is faith the same as religion? Can I have a relationship with God and reject Jesus? All of these and other similar questions plague humanity, because mankind in general wants to believe there are many ways to heaven, many ways to God.

Everyone, at some point in time, has asked themselves or given thought to, at least, one of these questions or one similar. Many of us will say we believe in God, or we believe in Christ or that we are a Christian. But if you really stop to examine your faith and what you understand about what you believe, you may be surprised, shocked and even dismayed. Yet this is exactly what must happen in your heart. To be made whole as Jesus said, the hole must be filled with the right packing.

I joined church at the age of fourteen and was baptized by immersion, and I thought I was good. But I still went to church every now and then just like before. I felt I was a decent person, doing as much good as I could, just like before. Being a people pleaser, I did all I could to make others happy, just like before. I prayed to God, during those times when I was in trouble or needed something, just like before.

I used God like a vending machine, just like most people. I called on Him to provide His stuff when I needed Him to and other than that, I left Him alone and He left me alone or so I thought. With all of that, I still felt empty in a place of my heart that I couldn't reach no matter how hard I tried. There is so much more to this story, but the point is I thought I was saved as a Christian and on my way to heaven because I went to church, knew about God, and had faith that He would do what I asked. When He didn't, then the type of faith I had was revealed as a ship without a rudder, tossed back and forth by the strong winds of the sea. As long as things were good, I was good, but when trouble came, my faith went. The Bible describes it as the wavering faith of a double-minded person, in the Book of James 1:6-8.

I was Wrong! I didn't really understand just how wrong I was until the year 1981. I was twenty-seven, had two children, working part-time and going to nursing school full-time. During that whole year, it was as though I felt death all around me and I was stifled with fear and anxiety. My daily life's circumstances were not a problem. I struggled through fairly successfully. But it was the life within me at war, and I was losing big time and couldn't figure out why.

I remember a day at my mother's house; a few of my sisters and I were gathered and I felt pressed to ask them if they felt the presence of death, as I gave them more details. I just knew I was going to die soon. Of course, they thought I was crazy, and to some degree, I did too. But this overwhelming presence of death didn't stop, instead, it seemed to get darker and deeper. I was having literal nightmares that seemed so real, where I struggled against demonic forces. These occurrences, fear, anxiety and depression drove me to start asking questions I thought I already knew the answers to. It started with me questioning my faith and what I knew about God. I began to identify with the Israelites in Exodus 19 and 20. I knew about God's works and thought I deserved His blessings and promises, wrong again.

It took me about another year or so just to try to understand what was going on, and why my faith and knowledge of God were even a question for me. Once I gave in to the possibility that I didn't have it all together,

God stepped in. In His infinite wisdom and compassion, He revealed to me that my problem and spiritual struggle was having faith in what I thought I knew about the God of my mind. So my faith was rooted in knowledge of who I thought God was and not the Person, Himself.

You can only come to know someone by entering into an intimate relationship with them, reading and studying their autobiography when there is one, and spending time learning what pleases them. God revealed to me, I had done none of those things. *WOW God!* I was so excited when I realized that God used all those horrors in 1981 to push me to let Him in.

The more I studied, prayed and meditated on Him and His word, I came to realize that God had even used every terrible thing that happened to me in years past to bring out something for His glory and for my good, which was to seek Him even more (see Romans 8:28). He was knocking down some barriers in my heart I didn't understand were there so He could come in and begin to make me whole.

Saving Faith is Required

So again, I say that the first and most important intervention for spiritual healing is to examine your faith. Ask yourself those questions you think you already have the answers to. Open up and let God expose you to yourself. When you are willing to accept that exposure and vulnerability, God can go to work for your good and on your behalf, for real. Only a repentant heart with faith and trust in who Jesus Christ is, what He did on the cross for us all, faith in His resurrection and His presence at the right hand of the Father, can fill the yearning in our spirits. Only faith and belief that the God of the Bible set this plan in motion before the foundation of the world, that all who come to Him by The Way would have eternal life and not perish, (see John 3:16). Being reconciled to God by grace through faith in Jesus Christ gives us spiritual life as we are reunited with the Spirit Father forever.

I learned that to get all God has for you, you've got to take all of who God is, and learn the ways of His character and nature which requires a relationship with Him. For this relationship to happen, we must come to God by grace through faith in Jesus Christ, just as He says we must do, (see Ephesians 2:8). We cannot earn God's love, His grace or His mercy. But in response to His love, we must desire and seek to become more like His Son. We must desire to please Him through our faith in Him, (see Hebrews 11:6).

There must be a foundation of faith and belief for holistic healing to take place in one's being. That framework includes:

- A belief that good and evil forces do exist in the world because of one man's action in the garden, Adam.

- Belief that Adam's choice to believe a lie rather than the truth of what God spoke and his actions that followed, spiritually separated all of humanity from a loving and compassionate God
- Belief that no human being could ever pay the debt owed to God for what Adam did against God
- Belief that the sin debt had to be paid by someone who qualified as pure enough to cover the full price God required
- Belief that without the debt being paid there would be no way for the relationship between God and man to be fixed or reconciled. Every human soul would be condemned forever, eternally separated from God.
- Belief that Jesus, God's only begotten Son, was the only person qualified to take care of that bill in full and He did it willingly out of love for you and me, on the cross at Calvary
- Belief that when Jesus died on the cross, God accepted His sacrifice of Himself as payment in full
- Belief that God raised Jesus from the dead three days after His death on the cross to seal the deal. It sealed away the power of sin over our lives
- Belief that Jesus lives and sits with the Father constantly interceding on our behalf
- Belief that Jesus died for you so you could live and have an intimate, loving relationship with God eternally

- Belief that Jesus' death provided the grace and mercy of God to show that God accepted His sacrifice and humanity is forgiven
- Accepting the Person and work of Jesus Christ; asking Him to come into your heart as Savior and Lord of your life
- Making this faith infrastructure the beginning of a belief system that will lead, guide and direct your path in life and in fellowship with God forever

We don't have all of the answers, and the man-made solutions are temporary, but the Lord is eternal! Either you create a temporary identity for yourself without Christ, or you can choose the everlasting identity that is found and secured by faith in Christ. Choosing to live a life in Christ guarantees us the indwelling presence of the Holy Spirit while we walk the paths of life. He guarantees us wholeness and help to make better choices, to love and not to hate, to forgive and be forgiven and to work at being at peace with all men, as much as possible. Hebrews 12:14 (NKJV) states, "Pursue peace with all people, and holiness, without which no one will see the Lord." The presence of the Holy Spirit guarantees that as we move into a right relationship with God and allow Him to transform us then what comes out of our heart, will be character traits produced by the Spirit as stated in Galatians 5:22-25 KJV,

"But the fruit of the Spirit is love, joy, peace, long-suffering, gentleness, goodness, faith, Meekness, temperance: against such there is no law. And they that are Christ's have crucified the flesh with the affections and lusts. If we live in the Spirit, let us also walk in the Spirit. Meekness, temperance: against such there is no law. And they that are Christ's have crucified the flesh with the affections and lusts. If we live in the Spirit, let us also walk in the Spirit."

d. Healed: Made Whole

What Happened with Zacchaeus as He Was Made Whole?

In the Gospel of Luke chapter 19, there is a Jew named Zacchaeus, who was a tax collector for the Roman government. He was so hated by his people because of his crooked, corrupt practices against his own people on behalf of the Roman government. He overcharged the people, so he could pay the Romans well, and line his own pockets to support his lavish lifestyle. Jewish tax collectors had no compassion or concern for their fellow brethren.

Zacchaeus may have been wealthy with the pleasures of material stuff and may have even seemed happy or content, but we find out something very different. We find out that he was not happy, that he had no real joy in his heart and probably didn't even realize it. Since he was of Jewish descent, he surely knew that the Messiah, a Savior, was coming based on Old Testament Scriptures. As Zacchaeus heard about this Jew that was going about the country healing all manner of diseases, giving sight to the blind, making the lame walk and raising others from the dead, he had to think this might be the One the Scriptures foretold of the One that was promised by God to come and save His people from the sin and oppressions of the world.

Luke 19:1-10 tells the event of Zacchaeus and his encounter with Jesus. He heard that Jesus was passing through town, and something began to stir in his heart. He may have thought, could this be Him, the One my ancestors told me about, the One that will deliver us from the oppression of the Roman government? As the heart of this wealthy tax collector started beating fast, maybe the palms of his hands got sweaty as he became emotionally excited, so much so, he couldn't contain it.

He was willing to consider the possibility that Jesus could do for Him what no other person could. Maybe he didn't realize what that something even was, at this point. Maybe he felt something missing in his heart, a void that he didn't know how to fix. He just knew he had to see this Man, Jesus. He lit out running as fast as he could to get ahead of the crowd moving in the direction he heard they were going.

Zacchaeus was a short man in stature, so while on the run, he saw a tree he could climb to see Jesus over the crowd. His heart was so stirred just at the hope of getting to see Jesus, that it moved him into a spiritual healing process. When Jesus saw and spoke to Zacchaeus, what an encounter it was. Zacchaeus was so convicted that his heart immediately began to regret all the crooked and corrupt practices he had done of cheating his people, the Jews. He regretted all his evil deeds against others in a godly sorrow, (see 2 Corinthians 7:10) and was moved to repent, making a fourfold restitution.

The same thing happened to Matthew, one of Jesus' disciples. He too was a tax collector whose heart was convicted and converted which led to his repentance of his corrupt practices. Matthew also walked away from his position of wealth and followed Jesus (see Matthew 9:9-13).

The problems of this world are spiritual, yet we experience them physically, mentally and emotionally even more. There are no laws of man that can change how people act because laws can't change a person's heart. There are no politicians who can enact a bill that will stop bigotry, prejudices or violence. There is no law that will stop parents from abusing children, spouses from abusing each other, or stop people from committing heinous crimes. There must be a change of the heart. There is no love great enough to make people stop being selfish and self-centered without the love of Christ as the life within. There is no way to have a relationship with God just by receiving the blessings He gives and the promises

He keeps because we only see His works. So we learn to trust in His works rather than His ways. You can only get to know God by getting to know His character, His nature and His ways. There is no spiritual life without an intimate relationship with the Spirit Father. Only then can there be true holistic healing otherwise there will always be a void in your life.

There are countless accounts of Jesus healing men and women throughout the New Testament, restoring them to a place of wellness, dignity and for some, prominence in society as only He can do. Let's hear from a few of them:

- **Mark 5:28-29 KJV -(The woman bleeding for 12 years)** "For she said, If I may touch but his clothes, I shall be whole, and straightway the fountain of her blood was dried up; and she felt in her body that she was healed of that plague"

- **Luke 8:38-39 NKJV -(The demon-possessed man)** "Now the man from whom the demons had departed begged Him that he might be with Him. But Jesus sent him away, saying, "Return to your own house, and tell what great things God has done for you." And he went his way and proclaimed throughout the whole city what great things Jesus had done for him.

- **John 9:10-12 NIV -(The blind man)** "How then were your eyes opened? They asked. He replied,

"The man they call Jesus made some mud and put it on my eyes. He told me to go to Siloam and wash. So I went and washed, and then I could see. Where is this man? they asked him. I don't know, he said."

- **Luke 17:14-16 NIV (The 10 Lepers)** "When he saw them, he said, "Go, show yourselves to the priests. And as they went, they were cleansed. [15]One of them, when he saw he was healed, came back, praising God in a loud voice. [16]He threw himself at Jesus' feet and thanked him and he was a Samaritan." Jesus healed all ten of them, but only the hated half-breed was actually grateful enough to thank Him.

Here are just a few of the people who testify of their healing, made whole by Jesus. There were some who believed them and some that didn't. People who really want to be made whole will accept the opportunity given in Jesus and others will always remain spectators and critics. Where do you fall?

When these men and women came to Jesus, they came acknowledging they had a problem that they could not fix, they came seeking Jesus' help with a problem that they had no clue of what the outcome should look like. They came to Jesus humbly believing He had the power to heal them, believing He had the compassion to heal them, so they trusted that He would heal them. There's no way to spend quality time with Jesus and not be changed. Holistic healing is an ongoing process needed until we get to our eternal destination. For some, it will be heaven and for others, it will be eternal torment because of eternal separation from God. We are given The Fathers' promises of full restoration (see Isaiah 61; Revelations 22).

We may not be able to control the decisions that people make to inflict terrible acts of abuse and violence on others, but as adults, we can control how those adverse experiences affect our lives, our relationships, and our intellectual abilities. We must take back control and charter a new course for who we are today and our relationship with God.

To be healed, to be made whole emotionally, mentally, and spiritually from past trauma, abuse, neglect, and maltreatment you must desire Jesus' help, have faith that He can do it, and trust that He will do it for you. As survivors, we no longer have to be slaves of our past or held captive by our own minds anymore. Luke 4:18 NKJV tells us that Jesus came to set the captives free, "The Spirit of the Lord is upon Me, because He has anointed Me to preach the gospel to the poor; He has sent Me to heal the brokenhearted, To proclaim liberty to the captives And recovery of sight to the blind, To set at liberty those who are oppressed;" so we are not destroyed. Survivors of any kind of trauma are the heirs of the greatest inheritance from God: hope, health, peace, love, joy, and redemption which must be realized through faith in God, the Father and Jesus Christ our Savior and Lord.

If you have not been made whole by grace through faith in Christ Jesus as Savior and Lord, won't you ask Him to come into your life and abide with you in your heart today? You can pray from your heart in your own words. God is more concerned with the motive and sincerity of the heart than the words from our mouths. You may also feel free to use this simple prayer as a guide.

"Dear God, I need You. I admit that I am a sinner. But, because You love me, You made a way for my debt to be paid, my sins to be forgiven and for me to be saved for eternal life with You. I believe that You sent Jesus Christ to die on that cross to pay the debt for my sin so I wouldn't have to. Jesus, thank You for taking the punishment in my place. I want You to come into my heart right now. Take control of my life and make me be the person You created me to be. Thank You for Your peace and unconditional love, I now receive in my heart. In Jesus Name – Amen"

Congratulations and welcome to God's eternal family. Now, join a church family rooted in God's truth to help nurture and encourage your spiritual growth and your walk with Jesus.

THE BEST IS YET TO COME!

Reference Page

1. Child Welfare Information Gateway. (2019). Long-term consequences of child abuse and neglect. Washington, DC: U.S. Department of Health and Human Services, Administration for Children and Families, Children's Bureau, viewed 2/14/22
https://www.childwelfare.gov/pubpdfs/
long_term_consequences.pdf

2. National Domestic Violence Hotline, viewed 7/16/22 at 11:55 am
www.thehotline.org/identity-abuse/understand-relationship-abuse/

3. Truth According to Scripture, Bible Commentary, Spurgeon's verse Exposition of the Bible
https://truthaccordingtoscripture.com/commentaries/spe/matthew-
15.php#.YtNmY3bMJPY viewed on 7/16/22 @, 8:35 pm
Child Welfare Information Gateway, State Statutes as of March 2019, Definitions of Child Abuse and Neglect,
https://www.childwelfare.gov/pubpdfs/define.pdf

5. Oxford Academy, International Journal of Epidemiology, article "Child abuse in 28 developing and transitional countries--results from the Multiple Indicator

Cluster Surveys by Manas K Akmatov, published 10/13/2010. Viewed 3/5/2022 https://academic.oup.com/ije/article/40/1/219/6612520

6. Child Welfare Information Gateway. (2021). Definitions of domestic violence. Department of Health and Human Services, Administration for Children and Families, Children's Bureau, 7/25/22. https://www.childwelfare.gov/topics/ systemwide/laws-policies/statutes/ defdomvio/

7. National Coalition Against Domestic Violence (2020). Domestic violence. Retrieved from https://assets.speakcdn.com/assets/2497/ domestic_violence-2020080709350855.pdf?1596811079991.

8. The American Society for the Positive Care of Children (American SPCC), site visited 2/25/22. https://americanspcc.org/child-maltreatment-statistics/

9. Centers for Disease Control and Prevention, "Research Brief: One billion children across the world are exposed to violence in childhood each year" https://www.cdc.gov/violenceprevention/ childabuseandneglect/vacs/onebillion-children.html

10. Siladitya RayForbes Staff, Business Article, October 5, 2021, viewed 3/3/2022 at . Ot https://www.forbes.com/sites/siladityarav/2021/10/OS/at -least-330000-minors-were-victims-of-sex-abuse-in-the-french-catholic-church-since-1950-report-finds/? sh=957e8af55662

11. The Washington Post, online article By Michelle Boorstein and Gary Gately, August 14, 2018. Viewed 3/3/2022 https://www.washingtonpost.com/news/acts-of-faith/wp/2018/08/14/pennsylvania-grand-jury-report-on-sex-abuse-in-catholic-church-will-list-hundreds-of-accused-predator-priests/?noredirect=on

12. PBS News Hour, "3 of U.S.'s biggest religious de-nominations in turmoil over sex abuse, LGBT policy", By David Crary, Associated Press Nation Mar 3, 2019 3:04 PM viewed 3/3/2022 https://www.pbs.org/newshour/nation/3-big-us-churches-in-turmoil-over-sex-abuse-lgbt-policy

13. Pew Research Center, viewed on 8/1/22 https://www.pewresearch.org/fact-tank/2018/11/20/americans-who-find-meaning-in-these-four-areas-have-higher-life-satisfaction!

14. Pew Research Center, viewed on 8/1/22 https://www.pewresearch.org/interactives/in-

their-own-words-how-americans-explain-why-bad-things
-happen/

15. Encyclopedia.com visited 3/5/2022,
https://www.encyclopedia.com/social-sciences/
encyclopedias-almanacs-transcripts-and-maps/spiritual-
crisis

16. PBS News Hour, "3 of U.S.'s biggest religious de-
nominations in turmoil over sex abuse, LGBT policy', By
David Crary, Associated Press Nation Mar 3, 2019 3:04
PM viewed 3/3/2022 https://www.pbs.org/newshour/
nation/3-big-us-churches-in-turmoil-over-sex-abuse-
lebt-policy

17. National Institue of Health, Pub Med, "The impact of
child sexual abuse on attitudes toward God and the
Catholic Church", online article By SJ Rossetti, viewed
3/3/2022 https://pubmed.ncbi.nlm.nih.gov/8777697/

18. Office of Disease Prevention and Health Promotion
(last updated 2/6/2022. viewed 8/23/22. A federal government website managed by the US Department of
Health and Human Services.

https://www.healthypeople.gov/2020/topics-objectives/
topic/mental-health-and-mental-

disorders#:~:text=Neuropsychiatric%20disorders%
20are%20the%20leading.to%20disability
%20and%20premature%20mortality.

19. Mental Health America National Organization,
https://www.mhanational.org/what-are=endorphins#27

20. Prepared by: Office of Communications and Public
Liaison, National Institute of Neurological Disorders and
Stroke, National Institutes of Health, Bethesda, MD, last
reviewed 7/25/22. https://www.ninds.nih.gov/health-
information/patient-caregiver-education/brain-basics-
know-your-brain#:~:text=The%20brain½20is%20the%
20most,movement%2C%20and%20controller%20
01%20behavior.

21. Free Wikipedia -on 9/13/22, https://en.wikipedia.org/wiki/
Cardiocentrichypothesis#:~:text=Aristotle%20observed%
20tha‡%20the%20heart.blood%20vessels%20to%20produce%
20sensation.

22. The History of the Heart, Stanford University website
https://web.stanford.edu/class/history13/earlysciencelab/
body/heartpages/heart.html

23. American Psychological Association, Dictionary of
Psychology, 9/29/22, https://dictionary.apa.org

24. U.S. Department of Health & Human Services, Office of population Affairs, visited 11/3/22 https://opa.hhs.gov/adolescent-health/reproductive-health-and-teen-pregnancy/trends-teen-pregnancy-and-childbearing

25. Content source: Division of Reproductive Health , National Center for Chronic Disease Prevention and Health Promotion Page last reviewed: November 15, 2021, visited 11/3/22
https://www.cdc.gov/teenpregnancy/about/index.htm
26. Merriam-Webster online dictionary. https://www.merriam-webster.com/dictionary

27. The New Strong's Expanded Exhaustive Concordance of the Bible, Red Letter Edition, by Thomas Nelson Publishers 2010.

28. Simply Psychology, Sigmund Freud's Theories, By Saul McLeod, updated 2018
https://www.simplypsychology.org/Sigmund-Freud.html

29. The 2023 Encyclopadia Britannica, Inc. The Britannica Dictionary, viewed 1/3/2023, https://www.britannica.com/dictionary/soul

30. American Psychological Association, viewed 1/5/23
https://www.apa.org/education-career/guide/subfields/social

31. Simply Psychology, What Is Social Psychology? Definition, Theories & Examples

By Dr. Saul McLeod, published 2007, 1/5/23, https://www.simplypsychology.org/social-psychology.html

32. Pew Research Center, visited 2/13/23, https://www.pewresearch.org/fact-tank/2018/04/25/key-findings -about-americans-belief-in-god/

33. Khan Academy https://www.khanacademy.org/science/biology/intro-to-biology/what-is-biology/a/what-is-life

SPIRITUAL CHECKUP

SPIRIT HEALTH AND WELL-BEING	
Where are you?	Check one
Rejecter – made the choice not to believe in the God of the Bible, therefore reject His offer of salvation by grace through faith in Jesus Christ	
Unbeliever-have not given much thought to understand or believing in the God of the Bible, Jesus Christ, or the Holy Spirit	
Seeker -giving the God of the Bible consideration, exploring the possibility of His truths	
Believer – have made the choice to accept the gift of salvation to eternal life by grace through faith in Christ Jesus, His Person, His work on the cross, His resurrection, and His ascension to the Father. Your faith says Jesus is the Giver of life, and you desire a close relationship with God, but you allow life to get in the way which can lead to struggles that makes it more difficult	
Follower – have learned how to fight with spiritual weapons to overcome some of life's challenges, refuse to settle for just being a believer and is growing as a disciple following the teachings of Jesus Christ	
Laborer – a believer, a follower and makes the mission of the Kingdom of God a priority in everyday life and strive to help others do the same	

It's A Matter of the Heart

Spiritual Health Questionnaire	Firmly Agree	Agree	Not Sure	Firmly Disagree
I read the Bible daily because it is important to me				
I pray daily because it is important to my life				
I am confident in my eternal destination for heaven				
Bible truths and values govern my decision making daily				
My daily schedule reflects a balance between family and work with God first				
I am increasingly aware of your own sin and seek God's forgiveness				
I am growing in love for those, in my life who makes it difficult for me to love them				
My lifestyle is noticeably difference than my peers who do not know and follow Jesus				
Being connected to a local church and being actively involved is important to me				
I actively seek to know God and His guidance on how to serve in His kingdom				
Family relationships are important to me, so I actively seek God's guidance on mending broken ones				
I struggle with forgiving those who have hurt me deeply				
I believe God wants us all to be happy and enjoy life				
I don't really believe in the God of the Bible, but I do believe there is a Higher Power in the universe				

Many modern believers have exchanged true faith in Jesus Christ for a pseudo-faith that resembles Christianity but is actually a dangerous counterfeit. There is a difference in having faith in our faith rather than faith in Jesus or having faith in what we know about Jesus rather than faith because we know Jesus. **WHERE DO YOU FALL**?

*Vital*signs™

CDC

#vitalsigns
NOV.2019

Adverse Childhood Experiences (ACEs)
Preventing early trauma to improve adult health

Want to learn more?
www.cdc.gov/vitalsigns/aces

1 in 6 — 1 in 6 adults experienced four or more types of ACEs

5 of 10 — At least 5 of the top 10 leading causes of death are associated with ACEs

44% — Preventing ACEs could reduce the number of adults with depression by as much as 44%.

Overview:

Adverse Childhood Experiences (ACEs) are potentially traumatic events that occur in childhood. ACEs can include violence, abuse, and growing up in a family with mental health or substance use problems. Toxic stress from ACEs can change brain development and affect how the body responds to stress. ACEs are linked to chronic health problems, mental illness, and substance misuse in adulthood. However, ACEs can be prevented.

Preventing ACEs can help children and adults thrive and potentially:

- Lower risk for conditions like depression, asthma, cancer, and diabetes in adulthood.

- Reduce risky behaviors like smoking, and heavy drinking.

- Improve education and job potential.

- Stop ACEs from being passed from one generation to the next.

PROBLEM:

Adverse Childhood Experiences impact lifelong health and opportunities.

ACEs are common and the effects can add up over time.

- 61% of adults had at least one ACE and 16% had 4 or more types of ACEs.

- Females and several racial/ethnic minority groups were at greater risk for experiencing 4 or more ACEs.

- Many people do not realize that exposure to ACEs is associated with increased risk for health problems across the lifespan.

Centers for Disease Control and Prevention
National Center for Injury Prevention and Control

Preventing ACEs could reduce a large number of health conditions.

UP TO	UP TO	UP TO
21 MILLION CASES OF DEPRESSION	**1.9 MILLION** CASES OF HEART DISEASE	**2.5 MILLION** CASES OF OVERWEIGHT/OBESITY

SOURCE: National Estimates based on 2017 BRFSS. Vital Signs. MMWR November 2019.

Potential reduction of negative outcomes in adulthood

HEALTH CONDITIONS

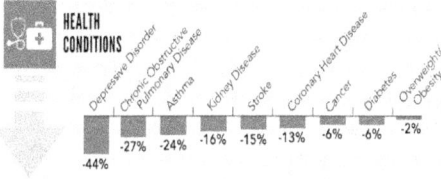

Depressive Disorder -44%, Chronic Obstructive Pulmonary Disease -27%, Asthma -24%, Kidney Disease -16%, Stroke -15%, Coronary Heart Disease -13%, Cancer -6%, Diabetes -6%, Overweight/Obesity -2%

HEALTH RISK BEHAVIORS

Current Smoking -33%, Heavy Drinking -24%

SOCIOECONOMIC CHALLENGES

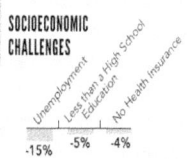

Unemployment -15%, Less than a High School Education -5%, No Health Insurance -4%

SOURCE: BRFSS 2015-2017. 25 states. CDC Vital Signs. November 2019.

Raising awareness about ACEs can help:

- Change how people think about the causes of ACEs and who could help prevent them.
- Shift the focus from individual responsibility to community solutions.
- Reduce stigma around seeking help with parenting challenges or for substance misuse, depression, or suicidal thoughts.
- Promote safe, stable, nurturing relationships and environments where children live, learn, and play.

THE WAY FORWARD >>>

HEALTHCARE PROVIDERS CAN:

- Anticipate and recognize current risk for ACEs in children and history of ACEs in adults. Refer patients to effective services and support.
- Link adults to family-centered treatment approaches that include substance abuse treatment and parenting interventions.

EMPLOYERS CAN:

- Adopt and support family-friendly policies, such as paid family leave and flexible work schedules.

STATES AND COMMUNITIES CAN:

- Improve access to high-quality childcare by expanding eligibility, activities offered, and family involvement.
- Use effective social and economic supports that address financial hardship and other conditions that put families at risk for ACEs.
- Enhance connections to caring adults and increase parents' and youth skills to manage emotions and conflicts using approaches in schools and other settings.

EVERYONE CAN:

- Recognize challenges that families face and offer support and encouragement to reduce stress.
- Support community programs and policies that provide safe and healthy conditions for all children and families.

http://go.usa.gov/xVvqD

For more information
1-800-CDC-INFO (232-4636)
TTY: 1-888-232-6348 | Web: www.cdc.gov

Centers for Disease Control and Prevention
1600 Clifton Road NE, Atlanta, GA 30333
Publication date: November 5, 2019

153

WHO ARE LICENSED PROFESSIONAL COUNSELORS

WHO ARE LICENSED PROFESSIONAL COUNSELORS?

Licensed professional counselors (or in some states, "licensed clinical professional counselors" or "licensed mental health counselors") provide mental health and substance abuse care to millions of Americans.

Licensed professional counselors (LPCs) are master's-degreed mental health service providers, trained to work with individuals, families, and groups in treating mental, behavioral, and emotional problems and disorders. LPCs make up a large percentage of the workforce employed in community mental health centers, agencies, and organizations, and are employed within and covered by managed care organizations and health plans. LPCs also work with active duty military personnel and their families, as well as veterans.

LPC QUALIFICATIONS

More than 120,000 professional counselors are licensed across the country, under licensure laws enacted in all 50 states, the District of Columbia, and Puerto Rico. LPC education and training standards for licensure are on par with those of the other two master's level mental health providers (clinical social workers and marriage and family therapists). State licensure requirements for professional counselors typically include:

- possession of a master's or doctoral degree in counseling from a national or regionally-accredited institution of higher education, including an internship and coursework on human behavior and development, effective counseling strategies, ethical practice, and other core knowledge areas;
- completion of a minimum of 3,000 hours of post-master's degree supervised clinical experience, performed within two years, and periodic com-

pletion of continuing education credits/hours after obtaining licensure;
- passage of the National Counselor Examination (NCE) or a similar state-recognized exam; and
- adherence to a strict Code of Ethics and recognized standards of practice, as regulated by the state's counselor licensure board.

WHAT DO LPCS DO?

The practice of professional counseling includes, but is not limited to, the diagnosis and treatment of mental and emotional disorders, including addictive disorders; psychoeducational techniques aimed at the prevention of such disorders; consultation to individuals, couples, families, groups, and organizations; and research into more effective therapeutic treatment modalities.

Counselors' training in the provision of counseling and therapy includes the etiology of mental illness and substance abuse disorders, and the provision of the well-established treatments of cognitive-behavioral, interpersonal, and psychodynamic therapy. Counselors' education and training is oriented toward the adoption of a truly client-centered, and not primarily illness-centered, approach to therapy.

Licensed professional counselors and members of the other non-physician mental health professions of psychology, clinical social work, marriage and family therapy, and psychiatric nursing provide the large majority of mental health services in the U.S. Roughly one in four Americans suffer from a diagnosable mental disorder in a given year, and about one in five Americans experience a mood disorder such as depression at some point in the course of their life.

AMERICAN COUNSELING ASSOCIATION

HOW TO FIND A LICENSED COUNSELOR

To search for a licensed counselor online, visit The Therapy Directory on the *Psychology Today* website at *http://therapists.psychologytoday.com/rms/*. You can search by zip code, area of specialty, and/or other criteria. Two other common ways to find a licensed counselor are by word-of-mouth and by looking in the yellow pages (typically under "counseling" or "counselors"; "marriage and family counseling"; or "mental health services"). Look for individuals who identify themselves as a "Licensed Professional Counselor" or "LPC." While some states have a variation of this title, the key words to look for are "licensed" and "counselor." Your state's counselor board website can let you know the specific designation in your state. Go to *http://www.counseling.org/Counselors/Licensure AndCert.aspx* to find a directory of state counselor licensure boards, including their phone number and internet address. Many state board web sites include search functions which let you verify the licensure of individual practitioners.

NEED FOR SERVICES

- 45.1 million adults (19.9%) in the United States had mental illness in the past year. Of those, nearly 8.9 million (20%) also had a substance use disorder.
- 11 million adults (4.8%) had serious mental illness (SMI)—a diagnosable mental disorder that substantially interfered with or limited one or more major life activities—in the past year.
- Less than 4 in 10 adults with mental illness in the past year received mental health services.
- In 2009, 14.8 million people (6.5% of adults aged 18 or older) had at least one major depressive episode during the past year.
- In 2009, 2 million youths (8.1% of the population aged 12 to 17) had at least one major depressive episode during the past year.

- In 2009, an estimated 8.4 million adults (3.7%) age 18 or older had serious thoughts of suicide in the past year. 2.2 million adults made suicide plans in the past year and approximately 1 million adults attempted suicide in the past year.

Substance Abuse and Mental Health Services Administration. (2010). *Results from the 2009 National Survey on Drug Use and Health: Mental Health Findings* (Office of Applied Studies, NSDUH Series H-39, HHS Publication No. SMA 10-4609). Rockville, MD.

AMERICAN COUNSELING ASSOCIATION

Copyright 2011
American Counseling Association

National Domestic Violence Hotline

FVPSA FACT SHEET

FYSB Mission

To support the organizations and communities that work every day to put an end to youth homelessness, adolescent pregnancy and domestic violence.

FVPSA Purpose

The Family Violence Prevention and Services Act helps states, territories, and tribes provide emergency shelter and supportive services to victims of domestic violence and their dependents.

Overview of Family Violence Prevention and Services Act Funding

The Family and Youth Services Bureau (FYSB), an office of the Administration on Children, Youth and Families at the Administration for Children and Families, administers funding through the Family Violence Prevention and Services Act (FVPSA) to ensure provision of emergency shelter and other non-shelter support services to address and prevent domestic violence and dating violence (42 U.S.C. § 10401-10414). Appropriated funds are allocated through three types of formula grants to states and territories, for distribution to local programs, to Tribes, and to state domestic violence coalitions. FVPSA also funds competitive discretionary grants to national, special issue, culturally specific, and emerging or current issue resource centers to provide training, technical assistance, and systems-based advocacy across the United States; and to a national domestic violence hotline. Generally, the FVPSA appropriation has been approximately $150 million, with an additional $8 million for the national domestic violence hotline.

The National Domestic Violence

HOTLINE

1.800.799.SAFE (7233) • 1.800.787.3224 (TTY)

The National Domestic Violence Hotline

The National Domestic Violence Hotline (The Hotline) is a compassionate, knowledgeable resource focused on shifting power back to those experiencing domestic or dating violence through human connection and practical help every day of the year. The Hotline offers immediate crisis counseling, emotional support, safety planning, and resources. Highly trained advocates provide warm referrals by directly connecting callers to local domestic violence shelters. For decades, The Hotline has served as FVPSA's national domestic violence hotline, providing services that are free, anonymous, and confidential.

The Hotline Special Projects

The StrongHearts Native Helpline launched in March 2017 between The Hotline and the National Indigenous Women's Resource Center (niwrc.org), a FVPSA-funded national training and technical assistance provider.

The National Domestic Violence Hotline, loveisrespect, and StrongHearts Native Helpline

Answered **323,081** total contacts in FY 17

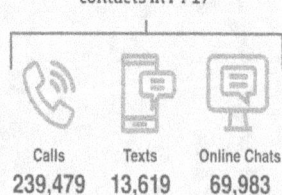

Calls	Texts	Online Chats
239,479	13,619	69,983

StrongHearts is a culturally relevant, safe, and confidential resource staffed by Native Americans for American Indian/ Alaska Native individuals experiencing domestic or dating violence.

Loveisrespect helps teens and 20-somethings learn about healthy relationships and dating violence. Advocates provide support, information, and advocacy to young people who have questions or concerns about their dating relationships, and can also help concerned parents, teachers, service providers, clergy and law enforcement understand how to address abuse among the young people they serve.

Services Provided	The Hotline	loveisrespect
Crisis Intervention	43.1%	25.5%
Safety Planning	37.2%	18.3%
Referral	34.8%	20.0%
DV Education	13.6%	10.3%
Healthy Relationships	7.9%	19.4%

Accessibility

The Hotline provides service referrals to agencies in all 50 states, Puerto Rico, Guam, and the U.S. Virgin Islands. Telephone and chat services are available in English 24 hours a day, every day of the year. Assistance is available from both English-speaking and Spanish-speaking advocates with access to more than 200 languages via a telephonic language line. Services are provided without regard to race, color, national origin, religion, age, sex, gender identity, sexual orientation, or disability (including deaf and hard of hearing).

Reach The Hotline

The Hotline

Tel: 1-800-799-SAFE(7233)
For Deaf and Hard of Hearing:
1-800-787-3224 (TTY)
1-855-812-1001 (Videophone)
Web: thehotline.org

StrongHearts Native Helpline

Tel: 844-7NATIVE (844-762-8483)
Web: strongheartshelpline.org

loveisrespect

Tel: 866-331-9474
For Deaf and Hard of Hearing:
866-331-8453 (TTY)
Web: www.loveisrespect.org
Text "loveis" to 22522

CONTACT US

Date updated: June 2018

Division of Family Violence Prevention and Services • **Web:** www.acf.hhs.gov/fvpsa
National Domestic Violence Hotline • **Tel:** 800-799-7233 • **Web:** www.thehotline.org

YOUR HEALTHIEST SELF

Social Wellness Checklist

Positive social habits can help you build support systems and stay healthier mentally and physically. Here are some tips for connecting with others:

MAKE CONNECTIONS

Social connections might help protect health and lengthen life. Scientists are finding that our links to others can have powerful effects on our health. Whether with family, friends, neighbors, romantic partners, or others, social connections can influence our biology and well-being. Look for ways to get involved with others.

To find new social connections:

☐ Join a group focused on a favorite hobby.

☐ Take a class to try something new.

☐ Try yoga, tai chi, or another new physical activity.

☐ Join a choral group, theater troupe, band, or orchestra.

☐ Help at a community garden or park.

☐ Volunteer at a school, library, or hospital.

☐ Participate in neighborhood events.

☐ Join a local community group.

☐ Travel to different places and meet new people.

TAKE CARE OF YOURSELF WHILE CARING FOR OTHERS

Many of us will end up becoming a caregiver at some point in our lives. The stress and strain of caregiving can take a toll on your health. It's important to find ways to care for your health while caring for others. Depending on your circumstances, some self-care strategies may be more difficult to carry out than others. Choose ones that work for you.

To take care of yourself while caring for others:

☐ Make to-do lists, and set a daily routine.

☐ Ask for help. Make a list of ways others can help. For instance, someone might sit with the person while you do errands.

☐ Try to take breaks each day.

☐ Keep up with your hobbies and interests when you can.

☐ Join a caregiver's support group.

☐ Eat healthy foods, and exercise as often as you can.

☐ Build your caregiver skills. Some hospitals offer classes on how to care for someone with an injury or illness.

Rev. Dr. Marilyn McClain

YOUR HEALTHIEST SELF | SOCIAL WELLNESS CHECKLIST continued

GET ACTIVE TOGETHER

Where you live, work, or go to school can have a big impact on how much you move and even how much you weigh. Being active with others in your community can have a positive effect on your health habits and create opportunities to connect. You can help your community create ways to encourage more physical activity.

To help make a more active community:

☐ Start a walking group with friends.
☐ Drive the speed limit and yield to people who walk.
☐ Consider joining an exercise group.
☐ Participate in local planning efforts to develop walking paths, sidewalks, and bike paths.
☐ Join other parents to ask for more physical activity at school.
☐ Try different activities!

SHAPE YOUR FAMILY'S HEALTH HABITS

Many things can influence a child, including friends, teachers, and the things they see when they sit in front of the TV or computer. If you're a parent, know that your everyday behavior plays a big part in shaping your child's behavior, too. With your help, kids can learn to develop healthy eating and physical activity habits that last throughout their lives.

To help kids form healthy habits:

☐ Be a role model. Choose healthy food and activities when together.
☐ Make healthy choices easy. Have nutritious food and sports gear readily available.
☐ Focus on making healthy habits fun.
☐ Limit screen time.
☐ Check with caregivers or schools to be sure they offer healthy food and activities.
☐ Change a little at a time.

BOND WITH YOUR KIDS

Parents have an important job. Raising kids is both rewarding and challenging. Being sensitive, responsive, consistent, and available to your kids can help you build positive, healthy relationships with them. The strong emotional bonds that result help children learn how to manage their own feelings and behaviors and develop self-confidence. Children with strong connections to their caregivers are more likely to be able to cope with life's challenges.

To build strong relationships with your kids:

☐ Catch kids showing good behavior and offer specific praise.
☐ Give children meaningful jobs at home and positive recognition afterward.
☐ Use kind words, tones, and gestures.
☐ Spend some time every day in warm, positive, loving interaction with your kids.
☐ Brainstorm solutions to problems together.
☐ Set rules for yourself for mobile devices and other distractions.
☐ Ask about your child's concerns, worries, goals, and ideas.
☐ Participate in activities your child enjoys.

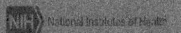

For other wellness topics, please visit www.nih.gov/wellnesstoolkits   NIH National Institutes of Health

159

It's A Matter of the Heart

BUILD HEALTHY RELATIONSHIPS

Strong, healthy relationships are important throughout your life. They can impact your mental and physical well-being. As a child you learn the social skills you need to form and maintain relationships with others. But at any age you can learn ways to improve your relationships. It's important to know what a healthy relationship looks like and how to keep your connections supportive.

To build healthy relationships:

☐ Share your feelings honestly.

☐ Ask for what you need from others.

☐ Listen to others without judgement or blame. Be caring and empathetic.

☐ Disagree with others respectfully. Conflicts should not turn into personal attacks.

☐ Avoid being overly critical, angry outbursts, and violent behavior.

☐ Expect others to treat you with respect and honesty in return.

☐ Compromise. Try to come to agreements that work for everyone.

☐ Protect yourself from violent and abusive people. Set boundaries with others. Decide what you are and aren't willing to do. It's okay to say no.

☐ Learn the differences between healthy, unhealthy, and abusive ways of relating to others. Visit www.thehotline.org/healthy-relationships/relationship-spectrum.

www.ingramcontent.com/pod-product-compliance
Lightning Source LLC
Chambersburg PA
CBHW071404120626
46546CB00002B/809